Fundraising with Businesses

Fundraising with Businesses

40 New (and Improved!) Strategies for Nonprofits

Joe Waters

WILEY

Cover Design: Paul McCarthy

Cover Image: © Getty Images/Eric Bean

Published by John Wiley & Sons, Inc., Hoboken, New Jersey.
Published simultaneously in Canada.

For general information on our other products and services or for technical support, please contact our Customer Care Department within the United States at (800) 762-2974, outside the United States at (317) 572-3993 or fax (317) 572-4002.

Wiley publishes in a variety of print and electronic formats and by print-on-demand. Some material included with standard print versions of this book may not be included in e-books or in print-on-demand. If this book refers to media such as a CD or DVD that is not included in the version you purchased, you may download this material at http://booksupport.wiley .com. For more information about Wiley products, visit www.wiley.com.

Library of Congress Cataloging-in-Publication Data:

Waters, Joe, 1967-
    Fundraising with businesses : 40 new and improved strategies for nonprofits / Joe Waters.
        pages cm. – (Wiley nonprofit authority series)
    Includes index.
    ISBN 978-1-118-61546-1 (cloth) – ISBN 978-1-118-61603-1 (ePDF) –
    ISBN 978-1-118-61572-0 (ePub) 1.   Fund raising. 2.   Social marketing.   I. Title.

    HV41.2.W38 2014
    658.15'224–dc23

                                                                    2013031244

Printed in the United States of America

10 9 8 7 6 5 4 3 2 1

To Deb, Cate, & Ryan

Contents

CONTENTS

Preface

This book is for all the nonprofit professionals who answered, "I don't know" when I asked them what type of fundraiser they would propose to a potential business partner.

Either they had a current business partner from whom they were only receiving a cash donation—always a good thing, but this pot of gold is getting smaller and is increasingly harder to find (see Chapter 9)—and had no other good ideas on how to raise money. Or they had no creative ideas for approaching a new business partner beyond asking for cash.

Stymied in their quest to raise money from businesses, these nonprofits let opportunities slip away until another nonprofit—usually a larger, national nonprofit—recruited the company and executed a successful fundraiser.

"They won over the business because they're a big nonprofit," they would rationalize.

"No," I'd reply. "They earned the business because they have know-how you don't. Just because you're small doesn't mean you have to *think* small."

This book aims to help nonprofits to think big about fundraising with businesses by expanding the opportunities for partnership.

If you're serious about training for a road race, what distance will you choose? Will you be a sprinter on the track? Or will you focus on something longer like a 10k or half-marathon? Maybe you'll set your sights on the ultimate endurance challenge, the marathon.

Knowing your options helps guide your training and sets the pace. If you plan to run a marathon, you won't spend your Sundays doing 50-meter track sprints. You'll be hitting the road for your long run.

But that's just what nonprofits do when it comes to working with businesses. They only have one strategy: ask them to write a check. But what if the business is small or new or struggling and doesn't have a lot of cash on hand? What if they want something for fundraising for you besides a thank you? What's your plan then?

Even more daunting is the company that *does* have money to give. Fixated on this one shiny nugget, nonprofits miss the treasure chest of donations that could be had from customers, employees or in shifting their focus from cash to in-kind products or services.

In whole, this book offers a new approach to fundraising with businesses. If you want to build a business giving program that is comprehensive, innovative and successful, you've come to the right place.

7 THINGS YOU SHOULD KNOW BEFORE YOU READ THIS BOOK

1. I don't use the term cause marketing. But that's what I'm talking about.

Even though *cause marketing* has been around since the early 1980s, most nonprofits—most people!—still don't understand what the term means. They think cause marketing means anything related to the *marketing of causes*, or to business giving in general.

On Twitter, I frequently see tweets that say, "Great example of cause marketing!" with a link to some clever piece of nonprofit marketing in print or video.

But I define cause marketing as *a partnership between a nonprofit and a for-profit for mutual profit*. The partnership is *win-win*. The nonprofit raises money and awareness and the for-profit earns a halo that enhances their favorability with consumers, which may increase sales.

Cause marketing partnerships are also *work-work*, which means neither partner gets a free ride. The nonprofit doesn't receive an unexpected check, and the for-profit doesn't write one expecting not to hear from the nonprofit for another year.

Good partnerships between a nonprofit and for profit are engaging, ongoing and valued.

After writing my first book *Cause Marketing for Dummies,* questions persisted on what exactly cause marketing was. I vowed not to use the phrase in my next book! That's how I ended up with *Fundraising with Businesses.* Just keep in mind that when you visit some of the resources connected with this book (e.g., my blog, Pinterest boards, etc.), you'll still see cause marketing in titles and posts.

Let's review: Cause marketing = Fundraising with Businesses

2. I'm inspiration. You're perspiration.

To be successful in anything you need inspiration. It's what drives us to keep pushing and excelling. Without it you just hit a dead end. You stop learning and exploring.

A key part of being inspired is feeling that what you're trying to achieve is doable.

Here's my own personal example:

Ten years ago, after a string of bad landscapers and gardeners, I decided I'd had enough. "Why can't I just do my own gardening and landscaping?" I asked myself. After a little research and reading a book, I was inspired that I could do it!

Today, I have one of the most beautiful yards on my street. (If you visit the Pinterest boards connected with this book you'll see I have the pictures to prove it!) Being a successful gardener involved a lot more than just reading a book. It took a lot of hard physical labor in both the heat and cold common to New England.

I hope this book gives you the same inspiration to tackle fundraising with businesses. Success will require plenty of perspiration, but what you're trying to grow is worthwhile and achievable. It will be something of which you'll be proud.

3. I'm focused on raising money from businesses.

I've worked for nonprofits for 20 years, and although I had plenty of different kinds of bosses during those two decades they all shared one thing: They all wanted to raise money.

This meant that regardless of what idea I hoped to execute with a business, it had to support the bottom-line of the organization. None of my bosses had the time or patience for testing concepts or trying new things just to try them.

It was frustrating at times because I had all these great new ideas bouncing around in my head. But my bosses were right. When it comes to raising money with businesses *if there is no profit there is no purpose.*

I brought the same thinking to this book. Although there are other ways for businesses to help nonprofits (e.g., volunteering, pro bono work), I focused on raising money. For example, I didn't write a chapter on volunteering, but I did write a chapter on Dollars for Doers programs, which reward volunteer hours with a company donation to the nonprofit.

The exceptions are chapters on collection drives and product donations. I spoke with nonprofits that benefited from these strategies and they assured me that in-kind items are as valuable as cash. Reflecting my preference for cold, hard cash, I nevertheless suggest some ways that you can turn the stuff from collection drives into cash for your organization.

We, of course, could have a spirited debate on why other types of business giving should be included in the book. But if you and/or your boss are bottom-line focused, I think you'll be happy with the 40 strategies I chose.

Remember, thanks to the online components of this book, we can add to my original 40. I expect this number to grow!

4. I talk a lot about point-of-sale programs.

As I reviewed the book for publication, I noticed I dedicated several chapters to point-of-sale fundraisers and mentioned them in many other places throughout the book.

Point-of-sale (POS) fundraisers are checkout programs that happen at the registers and involve a customer and a cashier. There are four types of POS fundraisers: donation boxes, register fundraisers, pinups, and round-up fundraisers.

I've dedicated a lot of words to POS fundraisers with good reason. Point-of-sale programs are the most lucrative type of business fundraiser.

PREFACE

As I'm writing this preface, I just learned that the antihunger organization Share Our Strength raised nearly $300,000 with a month-long pinup program with America's burger stand Shake Shack. The amount is staggering considering the money was raised from just 10 participating stores!

Nationally, these ask-to-give programs raise millions. The Cause Marketing Forum reported earlier this year that POS programs—or *checkout programs* as CMF calls them—raised a whopping $358 million in 2012. And this was just from the top 63 programs. Tens of millions of dollars more were undoubtedly raised from hundreds of regional and local POS fundraisers.

Point-of-sale fundraisers aren't appropriate for every type of business or nonprofit. That's one reason why I've given you dozens of alternatives to it. However, in businesses with multiple locations and long checkout lines, POS is a great place to start.

5. I don't talk about sponsorship.

You won't find a chapter on sponsorship in this book. I didn't write about it for three reasons.

First, the chapters in this book are around four to six pages long and I couldn't do justice to sponsorship with just one chapter. However, I had more reservations about writing on sponsorship than just page length.

Second, nonprofits probably know more about sponsorship than any other fundraising with business strategy. In the short space I had to write about sponsorship I'd be revisiting terrain with which nonprofits are familiar. In short, sponsorship isn't *new*, nor is there much to *improve*.

Third, sponsorship isn't the future of fundraising with businesses. With sponsorship, nonprofits solicit money from a company. In exchange, the nonprofit promotes the company at its events and/or programs (usually with signage, advertising or with program mentions).

But my argument in just about every chapter of this book is:

- There's more money in the company's employees and customers than there is the company checkbook, from which a nonprofit sponsorship would be underwritten.

○ Because the opportunity is with employees and customers, a sponsorship that exchanges cash for visibility among supporters at a nonprofit's annual dinner or walk generally misses the mark for everyone.

○ Sponsorship targets the wrong pot of money and what it funds (e.g. nonprofit events, programs, fundraisers, etc.) isn't as effective at delivering the "halo" that companies want for their financial support. The strategies highlighted in this book do.

6. I wrote this book for small nonprofits.

I only write about things I've done. I've never worked for a large nonprofit nor have I worked with big companies such as Starbucks, Target, or McDonald's.

I've worked for the local chapters of two voluntary health organizations. I sold memberships for a local chamber of commerce and underwriting for Boston's public television station. From 2004 to 2011 I was director of cause marketing for Boston's safety-net hospital.

Nearly every company I ever researched, cultivated, solicited, and recruited was located in eastern Massachusetts. The largest company I ever worked with was a discount retailer with 100 New England locations.

Having only worked for small nonprofits and with small to medium sized businesses, I wrote a book for fundraisers working in similarly sized organizations.

However, that doesn't mean that we can't learn something from our larger counterparts. I did all the time. A lot of the fundraising with business strategies they employ can be executed by smaller nonprofits in local areas. With the right training and realistic expectations of what a more modest effort can raise, small nonprofits can succeed.

7. Now is a great time for nonprofits to begin partnering with businesses.

The modern age of fundraising with businesses began in the early 1980s when American Express launched a fundraiser with its cardholders to restore The Statue of Liberty. It was the dawn of cause marketing.

I call the American Express campaign the "Columbus Moment," because, although cause marketing had been discovered and practiced before 1983 by the cause-pioneer Bruce Burtch in a partnership between Marriott Corporation and the March of Dimes, it was American Express that put this *new world* on the map—as Columbus did and not the Vikings, Chinese, or others who were thought to have visited the Americas before 1492.

Since the 1980s, cause marketing has been growing as a legitimate part of the marketing mix. First, at large companies, and now at the smaller companies that represent over 95 percent of the businesses in America.

Consumers are driving the rise of cause partnerships.

According to the 2010 Cone Cause Evolution Study—a full copy of which you can download from their website (www.coneinc. com)—consumers are being loud and clear in their expectations of companies.

- 90% of consumers want companies to tell them the ways they are supporting causes. In other words, 278+ million people in the United States want to know what a company is doing to benefit a cause.

- 83% of Americans wish more of the products, services, and retailers they use would support causes.

- Support for cause-related partnerships is especially strong (over 90 percent in favor) from two key consumer groups: moms (the household shoppers) and millennials (men and women born after 1980).

Smart businesses of all sizes are listening to consumers. Their reward is a competitive edge that goes beyond product and price. Although most forms of marketing are about *visibility*, cause marketing generates *favorability*.

Back in the early 2000s, when I talked with business owners, I had to explain what cause marketing was and how we could both benefit from a partnership. Today, businesses are well aware of company and cause partnerships and are aware of the benefits.

Instead of asking what cause marketing is, companies ask, "Which nonprofit should I work with?" "How should I work with them?"

You don't need to be a sales expert to know that these are great questions for prospects to be asking. The time is ripe for nonprofit and business partnerships. This book will give you the tools you need to succeed!

GETTING THE MOST OUT OF THIS BOOK

My hope for this book is that it will become your pocket guide for fundraising with businesses. Just as I refer to my copy of *National Audubon Society Regional Guide to New England* whenever I see a unique animal, bird, or insect in my yard, I want you to keep my book on hand whenever a potential business partner comes on your radar.

"Hmm . . . I wonder what fundraisers I should pitch this business? Let's see what Joe says in *Fundraising with Businesses*."

To help you identify that perfect strategy—or more likely *strategies*—this book also includes additional online content.

Pinterest

At the end of each chapter you'll find a URL and a QR code. When you visit the URL or scan the QR code you'll be directed to a Pinterest board with additional examples of the strategy.

If you are unfamiliar with QR codes and how to use them, there is plenty of free information online on how to download a QR code scanner on your mobile device and how to use it. If you're interested in learning more about QR codes, I wrote a whole book on them: *QR Codes For Dummies*.

Along with QR codes, Pinterest is one of my favorite digital discoveries. This virtual pin board has grown remarkably over the past few years. It's now the third largest social networking site after Facebook and Twitter.

For most "pinners" (as we're called),—Pinterest is aspirational. We pin the things we aspire to for our lives, home, children, and so forth.

Soon after trying Pinterest, however, I realized it was a great place to curate the cause marketing campaigns I admired.

For this book, I created a Pinterest board for each chapter. Each board has a title that begins with the hashtag for the book, #fwb40, and then the chapter title. For example, the Pinterest board "#FWB40—Cause Products" goes with Chapter 13 on cause products. So, after reading this chapter, you can visit the URL or scan the QR code to visit the board.

Remember these two things. First, the URL's at the end of each chapter are *case sensitive*. This means you have to type them in exactly as they are shown or you'll get an error message instead of the board you're looking for. Second, you can always bypass the chapter specific URL and QR code by visiting http://pinterest.com/joewaters. Scroll through the boards until you find the one you are looking for.

I populated these boards with pins while writing the book, and I plan to continue adding content long after it's published, bought, and read by you! Adding a digital component to the book means an ongoing education on good fundraisers after which you can model your own.

Twitter

Do you use the microblogging social networking site Twitter? If you do—or if I can encourage you to join and use Twitter—we'll have another way to communicate with each other about *Fundraising with Businesses*.

I'm an avid Twitter user, and have been for nearly five years. It's a fabulous place to learn and to stay connected with thought leaders and, of course, friends. My handle on Twitter is @joewaters (http://twitter.com/joewaters).

Thanks to the miracle of hashtags. we can stay in contact about the book. The book's hashtag is #fwb40. The # symbol, called a hashtag, is used to mark keywords or topics in a Tweet. By using Twitter Search (https://twitter.com/search), and a variety of other online services (I use TweetDeck), you can follow tweets that use this hashtag.

I plan to use the hashtag #fwb40 to highlight topics of interest to readers of the book. It could be a great example of a new campaign, a pin I added to one of the book's Pinterest boards, a post that I wrote that is book-related or to even announce that I found fundraising with business strategy number 41!

The point is that Twitter is a great way for us to stay connected while you are reading and using the book. I'll answer as many questions as I can. More likely, however, following the hashtag will introduce you to additional content that will enhance your learning.

SelfishGiving.com

I post regularly on my blog Selfish Giving (http://selfishgiving .com). One of those posts is usually a podcast—*CauseTalk Radio*—I co-host with Megan Strand from Cause Marketing Forum. Selfish Giving is all about fundraising with businesses so the content there will always be relevant to this book.

You also have the option at my site to subscribe to my e-mail newsletter, which goes out bi-monthly. My newsletter features an original post, and a full listing of other posts I've written for such online sites as *Huffington Post Impact* and Razoo's *Inspiring Generosity*.

Subscribing to my newsletter is the best way to stay abreast of everything I'm writing about fundraising with businesses.

Acknowledgments

Few books are written alone. This one certainly wasn't. When I first conceived the book I knew I would need a lot of help. I had only worked directly with a dozen or so of the strategies, and was familiar with maybe another 10. I would need the help of others to reach my goal of 40 strategies!

Throughout the book, I've tried to note the contributions of others to different chapters but I want to thank several people in particular.

Carol Cone (aka "The Mother of Cause Marketing") originally suggested that I write a book on fundraising with businesses when I met with her at her Boston office in 2009. Her suggestion stuck with me. And, as they say, the rest is history. Thanks, mom!

Megan Strand of the Cause Marketing Forum helped me flesh out the initial idea of the book, and offered her insights at many points when I was stuck or needed guidance. Megan's boss, CMF founder and president Davie Hessekiel, has been a constant source of inspiration, guidance and support. Thank you, David.

I want to thank my mentor and friend Curt Weeden for allowing me to lean on his expertise and excellent book *Smart Giving Is Good Business* for my chapters related to corporate giving. Curt also allowed me to experiment with and learn from the nonprofits that participate in his thrice-yearly *New Strategies Forum* in Charleston, South Carolina.

Joanna MacDonald, the co-author of my first book, *Cause Marketing for Dummies*, offered valuable insights and suggestions based on her practical experience as a seasoned cause marketer at a Boston hospital.

Jessie Sherrer of Washington, DC-based Share Our Strength and Mollye Rhea of Atlanta-based For Momentum were helpful in identifying strategy ideas for the book, especially when I was down to my last two chapters!

ACKNOWLEDGMENTS

I owe a big debt of gratitude to the team at Wiley. Claire New, Susan McDermott, Jennifer MacDonald and Tula Batanchiev were helpful throughout the process—even after Superstorm Sandy all but leveled their offices in Hoboken, New Jersey.

As my main contact, Jennifer MacDonald was particularly thoughtful, helpful, understanding and, above all, patient. Thank you, Jen.

I'm also grateful to Amy Fandrei at the Wiley *For Dummies* division for the introduction to the nonprofit book team in Hoboken.

Copy editor Janet Burke was a big help in preparing the manuscript for publication.

I did a good part of my writing at the Starbucks in Newtonville, Massachusetts. The team there is a wonderful group of professionals led by store manager Carrie O'Neil. Their cheerfulness—and caffeine—fueled my writing.

My family—my wife Deb, children Cate and Ryan, and dog Charlie—also helped with the book.

After her own long work day, Deb would help me rewrite a sentence or paragraph that wasn't hitting the mark.

Cate always had a good suggestion when it came to choosing the right word, and Ryan was always there to refresh me with a question or an episode of *SpongeBob SquarePants*.

My Yorkie, Charlie, was literally by my side when I wrote the book. Although asleep most of the time, I'm sure he was dreaming of my success.

SpongeBob knew that writing was hard, lonely work. His friend Patrick asked, "SpongeBob, this pencil is broken. Why won't it make words?"

"Patrick, you have to think of the words yourself," SpongeBob explained.

My family makes my words possible. These words are for them: I love you.

CHAPTER ONE

Percentage-of-Sales Fundraiser

Percentage-of-sales (POS) programs with businesses are one of the more common and lucrative types of fundraisers. They're especially popular in October during Breast Cancer Awareness Month. During "Pinktober," some of the largest companies in the United States donate to breast cancer charities when consumers purchase specially marked products.

The percentage or portion of sales donated to charity varies by company and promotion, but the dollars can really add up. Although McDonald's donates just a penny from the sale of each Happy Meal, it raises millions of dollars for the Ronald McDonald House Charities, an independent nonprofit organization that provides a homelike environment for families with critically ill or injured children who must travel to receive health care.

With over 34,000 locations worldwide, McDonald's sells a lot of Happy Meals! Your business partner may not span the globe like McDonald's does, but a well-executed POS program of just about any size will make you smile.

BOSTON BAKES FOR BREAST CANCER

Carol Brownman Sneider never wanted her daughter to go through what she and her mother went through.

Carol was 16 when she lost her mother to breast cancer. It was the 1970s and people didn't openly talk about cancer. They called it

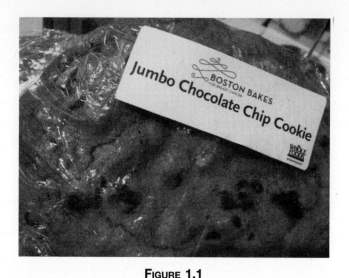

FIGURE 1.1

Boston Bakes for Breast Cancer

Source: Courtesy of Boston Bakes for Breast Cancer.

the "C" word. No one talked about it, including Carol's mother. She struggled and suffered in silence.

Carol wanted something different for her daughter and for every woman. In 1999, she started Boston Bakes for Breast Cancer.

Every spring, Carol canvases Greater Boston asking restaurants, bakeries, and cafes to choose a featured desert from which 100 percent of the proceeds benefit Boston Bakes. See Figure 1.1.

"A small business can only have so much of an impact by itself," said Carol. "Boston Bakes allows them to join nearly 300 other small businesses in a large program that's having a real impact."

To date, Boston Bakes has raised $1.75 million for its Boston charity partner the Dana-Farber Cancer Institute.

HOW IT WORKS IN 1-2-3

1. Working with your business partner, identify a product or service from which you'll receive a percentage or portion of sales.

2. Determine the percentage or portion you'll receive and for how long. It's also smart to set a maximum donation. For example, a local salon will donate $5 (up to a total donation of $500) from each haircut for the next three Saturdays.

3. Set an end date for the program and another date for when you can expect an accounting of donations and a check from the business owner.

THINGS TO REMEMBER

- To drive donations, choose a product or service that will be popular with customers. It should be one of the business's signature offerings. Every business knows what does and doesn't sell. Make sure you're getting a percentage from what does.

- The business is responsible for tracking sales of the item from which you'll receive a percentage. Depending on the business, you can ask for reports and spreadsheets of sales activity. With most small businesses, however, you'll have to trust the business owner and take his word for it.

- It's a good idea to cap your donation at a certain amount, especially if this is your first program together. Working with your business partner you can choose a total donation that is fair and generous. For example, during October, a bakery may agree to donate 50 cents from the sale of each blueberry muffin—a customer favorite—to a maximum donation of $250.

- Many businesses will agree to a minimum donation in case the percentage offered is too low or the product or service doesn't sell as expected. Our baker in the preceding point, for instance, may agree to donate $200 regardless of how many muffins are sold.

- Be clear to customers and supporters on how much will be donated from each sale, and who will get the money. How much of a portion of the purchase price will be donated?

To which organizations will the money be given? You want your fundraiser to be positive and successful, and not the latest example of bad fundraising practices.

- After the program, carefully review the results with your business partner. Did customers respond favorably to it? Did the business owner notice an uptick in business because of it? Was the dollar amount too low? Do you need to adjust the percentage received from each sale, or increase the maximum donation?

Transparency Should Be a Key Feature of Your Fundraiser

The fact that Breast Cancer Awareness Month is the most popular time of year for business fundraisers also makes it a lightning rod for critics that complain that these programs aren't transparent enough for consumers.

In the fall of 2011, the New York Attorney General issued guidelines entitled "Five Best Practices for Transparent Cause Marketing." (As I explained in the introduction, "cause marketing" is another term for "fundraising with businesses.") The practices include:

- **Clearly describe the promotion.** Explain which charity is benefiting from the program, how much they will receive, what consumers must do to trigger the donation and the minimum donation, if there is one. You should also include a start and end date for the promotion.
- **Be open about how much is being donated.** The guidelines suggest a donation label with this information.
- **Tell people what they need to know.** Is the company making a flat donation instead of a donation for each
(continued)

■ 4 ■

sale? Does the campaign have a cap, a maximum the business will donate?

- **There are no exceptions.** Transparency should extend to any online fundraising promotions as well. Traditional and digital campaigns should be equally transparent.

- **Tell the public how much was raised.** With all the digital tools we have access to these days, trying isn't good enough. Use offline and online media to let people know how much each fundraiser raised.

Following these guidelines will ensure that consumers stay focused on raising money for your organization, instead of raising questions about the legitimacy of your efforts.

STEAL THESE IDEAS!

1. You can create a percentage-of-sale program with *anything*. I've seen the program done with donuts, massages, and even rented spaces in a parking garage. Use your imagination and let your partner's generosity be your guide. Contemporary dance company Trey McIntyre Project partnered with a Boise-based tavern to raise funds from drinks named after dancers in the company. Get creative!

2. Combine a percentage-of-sale fundraiser with another fundraising idea from this book. For example, you can include a pinup or coin canister fundraiser to complement the campaign.

3. Avoid making the program overly complicated. When consumers are searching for products or services you only have a few seconds to connect with them. If they don't quickly understand the offer and how they can help, they'll most likely pass on it.

4. Copy Boston Bakes and recruit a group of similar businesses from which you can ask for a percentage. There's efficiency in having more businesses involved in the same effort, not to mention the added visibility and money you'll generate. In this case, bigger is better.

FOR MORE INFORMATION

 You can see more examples of percentage-of-sales programs by visiting http://fwb40.us/15t9kvJ or scan the QR code to view them on your smartphone or tablet.

CHAPTER TWO

Register Fundraiser

Cash registers have been a part of American business since after the Civil War. In addition to thwarting thieves, cash registers helped business owners track sales and manage inventory. They also gave rise to the checkout line, which business owners seized on to sell shoppers everything from candy to magazines to lip balm.

It was only a matter of time before pamphlets, signs, coin canisters, and other things supporting good causes also became a mainstay at the register. Businesses and nonprofits learned that when consumers had their wallets open, they were also willing to open their hearts to helping good causes.

WHOLE FOODS SUPPORTS NONPROFITS AT THE REGISTER

With over 300 locations nationwide, there's a good chance you've shopped at Whole Foods, an upscale chain of natural and organic food supermarkets based in Austin, Texas. Register fundraisers are a regular part of the Whole Foods checkout line. Every month, a different cause is featured and shoppers can donate a dollar or more.

Whole Foods promotes the cause of the month at the register— usually with signage on the credit card machine. Shoppers can support the YMCA by choosing $2 or $5 cards, which are affixed to the sign with Velcro. The cashier rings in the donation and returns the card to the sign for the next customer.

Most of Whole Foods' register fundraisers are passive, meaning the cashier doesn't ask the consumer to contribute. The shopper decides for herself how much to give, if anything.

Whole Foods register fundraisers are popular with nonprofits and with good reason. The Whole Foods Market in my town hosted a register fundraiser for the YMCA and raised $1,000. The amount raised varies from store to store, but when you multiply the results across the country Whole Foods raises a lot of money for charities with register fundraisers.

HOW IT WORKS IN 1-2-3

1. Using a register sign or tent, the business owner asks shoppers at checkout to donate to a nonprofit.
2. The shopper chooses the amount they want to donate. Sometimes they only have one choice (a dollar is common), but sometimes there are two or more choices ranging from $1 to $5.
3. The cashier collects the donation from the shopper and uses the businesses' point-of-sale system to record the donation.

THINGS TO REMEMBER

- Whether you use a sign or tent, put it where shoppers can't miss it. Smart businesses affix it right to the credit card machine so shoppers are sure to see it when they swipe their credit and debit cards.
- Be mindful of the size of the sign or tent. Businesses have limited space at the register and want to avoid "counter clutter" or anything that would turn off shoppers.
- An increasingly popular option is to include the donation request right on the screen of the credit card terminal. Some businesses even require that you donate or decline before completing your transaction. See Figure 2.1.
- Make sure you are clear on how the business will track donations. Every business has a point-of-sale system—a way of tracking sales. Use this same system to track donations.

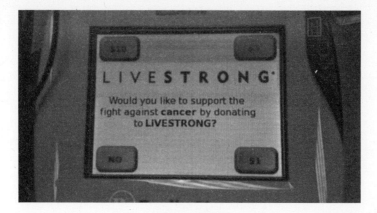

FIGURE 2.1

Donating via Credit Card Machine

Four Ways to Track Donations from Register Fundraisers

1. **Barcodes:** It's hard to imagine a time when retailers didn't have barcodes to scan and track products. Thankfully, they make processing and tracking donations a snap. Working with your business partner to produce a barcode isn't complicated, but timing is important. Be sure you have agreed on a barcode before anything is printed or distributed to the business partner. Reproducing materials can be expensive!

2. **Register Button:** If your business partner is a restaurant, bar or bakery, they can dedicate a button on the register for the donation. Work with the business to educate cashiers on where the button is on the register and what happens when they press it.

3. **Purchase Code:** Sometimes businesses will instruct cashiers to enter a purchase code for the donation.
   (continued)

(*continued*)
As with barcodes and a register button, this will allow the donation to appear on the shopper's receipt along with the other items purchased.

4. **Separate Envelope:** Smaller businesses without barcodes or a modern register can separate donations from purchases with a clearly marked envelope kept near the register. For security and tracking purposes, this isn't the best option. You can make the process more secure by reviewing the procedure with employees and scheduling frequent pickups.

STEAL THESE IDEAS!

1. Consumers that support register fundraisers sometimes have more questions about the fundraiser than the cashier has answers. It's a good idea to include a phone number, web page, or even a QR code on the register sign that will give consumers more information, if requested. Most consumers are quick to use the camera on their smartphones to capture information that is important to them.

2. For the reason mentioned earlier, signs should be mobile friendly. Use larger fonts and highlight key information. Test the signage with several different types of smartphones to make sure shoppers can easily read the sign after they snap a picture of it.

3. Although register fundraisers don't usually include an "ask" from the cashier, you'll raise more money if they do. See Chapter 15 on pinups and how getting cashiers involved can raise more money for your organization.

4. Raising money at the register is just one option. You can ask shoppers to sign a petition, take a pamphlet, watch a very brief video or join you at an upcoming event. You have their attention! Do something with it.

5. Register fundraisers can raise a lot of money. Focus on businesses with multiple locations and heavy foot traffic. The more locations and shoppers a business has, the more money you'll raise.

FOR MORE INFORMATION

 You can see more examples of register fundraisers by visiting http://fwb40.us/18JVYhK or scan the QR code to view them on your smartphone or tablet.

CHAPTER THREE

Donation Box Fundraiser

Donation boxes are one of the most common and most maligned fundraisers with businesses. They're easy to execute. All you need is a can with a coin slot. However, fundraisers and businesses counter that donation boxes are just counter clutter.

As one nonprofit executive explained to me: "They don't raise a lot of money and they're just kind of a hassle. Coins are heavy!"

I think the donation box has gotten a bad rap. Used in the right way with the right business—and shown some love—these simple fundraisers can collect thousands of dollars for your nonprofit.

BAGEL CHAIN COLLECTS CHANGE FOR SICK KIDS

My donation box program with Boston-based Finagle-a-Bagel started after another program failed. We tried pinups (see Chapter 15), but the program didn't do well.

The owners of Finagle, Laura Trust and her husband Alan Litchman, suggested donation boxes. They had used them with another nonprofit and had raised good money. But the charity, a well-known Boston nonprofit that raised a couple of hundred million dollars a year, decided to can the program. It was too much heavy lifting for a big-time charity. But not for me!

Laura and Alan and the whole team at Finagle embraced the program. They invested in sturdy donation boxes for their stores and put them front and center on the counter where customers couldn't miss them. And because they were locked in the back and

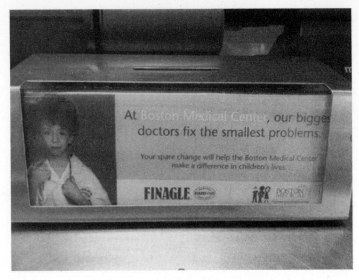

FIGURE 3.1

Finagle-a-Bagel's donation boxes

Source: Courtesy of Finagle-a-Bagel.

bolted to the counter, these donation boxes weren't going anywhere. See Figure 3.1.

Finagle was a perfect business for donation boxes. With the average tab being just a few dollars, customers paid in cash and had change leftover to donate. In just 14 months, they raised $25,000 for my nonprofit. That's a lot of coins for change!

HOW IT WORKS IN 1-2-3

1. The business partner agrees to add donation boxes to the register area.

2. The nonprofit or business owner invests in the donation boxes and both partners promote the program.

3. The nonprofit and the business agree on a schedule to pick up the coins.

THINGS TO REMEMBER

- Donation boxes work best in businesses that have lots of foot traffic from customers that pay with cash. Remember, you're targeting shoppers' spare change. There won't be any if customers are paying with checks or credit cards. Yes, you can put donation boxes in a car dealership, but how many car buyers pay with cash and get back change to drop in a donation box?

- Donation boxes don't work well in businesses where employees have a "tip jar" Employees won't appreciate customers donating instead of tipping and your donation box will soon be pushed aside.

- Donation boxes should be placed as close as possible to the register. A coffee shop near my house has a tip jar at the register and donation boxes at a separate counter where you get your napkins, cream, and sugar. Can you guess which one is chock full of money?

- Make security a priority with donation boxes. Stolen boxes will demoralize everyone. Secure the donation box to the counter or empty it frequently so it doesn't become a target for thieves.

Does Incentivizing Employees Produce a Better Fundraiser?

I'm convinced that incentivizing employees involved in a business fundraiser will raise a nonprofit more money. But don't just take my word. Ask Bryan Harding, Director of Cause Marketing at The Nature Conservancy, who has also seen the power of employee incentives. In an e-mail to me, he wrote:

(*continued*)

(*continued*)

> I can tell you with absolute certainty training and incentivizing employees for a round-up at the register or pin-ups makes a dramatic difference. Prior to The Nature Conservancy, I ran the cause marketing program at PetSmart Charities and the cause program at the American Heart Association National Center.
>
> At PetSmart, we had an in-store giving program with an at-register pin pad—it raised almost $30 million per year. We did test on with and without training and with and without incentives for employees across a network of over 1,000 stores—it worked much better when employees were trained and had incentives.

I've experimented with employee incentives for years and this is what I've learned.

Unmotivated employees stay unmotivated. Even with incentives unmotivated employees won't push the program.

Motivated employees don't need incentives. These employees support the program because they want to. They're motivated and disciplined and listen to their hearts, and to their manager. However . . .

Motivated employees can be *marginally* motivated with incentives. Incentives can give motivated employees an extra boost to push the program. But you don't need to give them much. A $5 gift card to a favorite coffee or sub shop will do the trick. So does a pizza party for the winning store at the end of the program.

Here are three more things you should know about incentives:

1. **You don't need to pay for incentives.** Getting incentives donated by various companies is easier than you think. You'll be amazed what you can get when you just ask for it.

2. **If this is your first fundraiser with a business, wait to offer incentives.** See how the first program goes and
(*continued*)

the type of employees you're working with. If the program does well, add the incentives to the next program to build on your success.

3. **Sometimes the best incentive for store employees is an easy-to-execute program.** Cashiers have enough to do and are probably already asking customers if they need batteries, want to apply for a store credit card, and so on. The last thing they need is a complicated program to push.

STEAL THESE IDEAS!

1.   Putting the donation box near the register isn't the only way to make it standout with shoppers. The USO and Kangaroo Express convenience stores turned their donation box program for America's military into a customer event. See Figure 3.2. Patriotic show cars visited stores and customers gave thanks to troops with recorded messages aired on the Salute Our Troops website at www.KESalute.com.

2.   You've probably heard the words "Trick or Treat for UNI-CEF!" Kids have been asking for candy for themselves and cash for UNICEF on Halloween for over 60 years. Launch your own donation box program for Halloween or another holiday when kids are visiting family, neighbors, and other potential donors. Recruit a business partner to underwrite the program and to distribute boxes to employees and customers.

3.   This past year, Merry Maids, the housecleaning service, brought something else with them besides brooms, mops, and cleaners when they visited their clients. They also brought a donation box, which they encouraged their clients to fill with coins during the month of February, American

FIGURE 3.2

Kangaroo Express Supports Its Donation Box Program with Store Events

Source: Courtesy of North Carolina National Guard via Flickr.

Heart Month. At the end of the month, Merry Maids employees collected the boxes and delivered the money to the American Heart Association. In its first year, the program raised $100,000.

FOR MORE INFORMATION

 You can see more examples of donation box fundraisers by visiting http://fwb40.us/17qzG6e or scan the QR code to view them on your smartphone or tablet.

CHAPTER FOUR

Hashtag Fundraiser

According to Twitter, "The # symbol, called a hashtag, is used to mark keywords or topics in a Tweet. It was created organically by Twitter users as a way to categorize messages."

Hashtags are an easy way to track a keyword or phrase (e.g. #nonprofit #corpgiving, #sandyrelief). Searching for or selecting a hashtagged word will link you to other Tweets that share the same hashtag. You can search for and track hashtags on Twitter Search (search.twitter.com).

Shortly after Twitter launched in 2006, businesses began using hashtags to donate money and products to good causes whenever social media users included a designated hashtag.

Twitter itself has held many hashtag fundraisers. In late 2012, Twitter offered to donate $1 in *Twitter Ads for Good* to the American Red Cross to promote their crisis relief efforts for each time #Tweet4-Good was shared before December 31. Twitter capped the donation at $20,000.

Hashtags are quickly becoming the most common way to group conversations around a topic on Twitter, Facebook, Instagram, Google+ and Pinterest. Hashtags are the emerging tool for social media fundraising between businesses and nonprofits.

SUPERMARKET DONATES 1,000—MAKE THAT 10,000— MEALS WITH HASHTAG CAMPAIGN

Over the holidays in 2012, global supermarket chain Lidl offered to donate five four-course Christmas dinners to food banks in

Belgium for each tweet with the hashtag #luxevooriedereen, which is Dutch for "luxury for everyone."

Unfortunately, the company was caught off guard when the promotion went viral, meaning that the hashtag spread rapidly on Twitter. This can be a good thing, but not for Lidl, which had privately committed to only donating 1,000 meals. Nevertheless, Lidl took the experience in stride and generously increased its donation to 10,000 meals.

The lesson for you is that when it comes to hashtag fundraisers, and social media in general, you have to plan for the unexpected and be clear on your maximum donation.

HOW IT WORKS IN 1-2-3

1. Working with your business partner, pick a unique hashtag and decide what will be given—cash or product—when people use it.

2. Chose a beginning and ending date for the campaign and cap the donation at an amount that is challenging but realistic.

3. At the end of the program, use Twitter search—or one of the many other online hashtag services—to track the number of hashtags and collect your donation.

THINGS TO REMEMBER

- Hashtag fundraisers work best when either the nonprofit or the business (preferably both) already have a sizable following on Twitter or another social network. It's difficult to put a number on what's *sizable*. Start by answering these questions: Are you active on Twitter or do you just have an account? Do you tweet at least a dozen times a day? Do you get your news, information and entertainment from Twitter and other social networking sites? If you answered yes, you may have the critical mass needed for a hashtag fundraiser.

- Choose a hashtag that's simple, but make it specific and unique. If you're a food pantry in Boston, for example, try #BFD13, which is short for "Boston Food Drive 2013."

- Promote the hashtag fundraiser everywhere, especially on other social networks (e.g. Facebook, Pinterest, web site), including Twitter.

- With a little exploring online you can find alternatives to Twitter Search to track the results of your campaign. I'm currently experimenting with Tagboard.com, which bills itself as the "Hashtag Hub." Regardless of what you use, make it a point to record the results weekly, if not daily. Twitter search tools limit results by date or number or both. If you wait until the end of your campaign, you may never know just how many times the hashtag was used.

- An alternative to tracking tweets is to secure an upfront and guaranteed donation from the company. Be sure to disclose this in the not-so-fine print (e.g., "ACME Company is donating $10,000. But your tweet still counts! Show your support for the campaign by tweeting the hashtag).

Twitter: Your Go-To Source for News on Business Giving

I used to read three daily newspapers and a bunch of magazines to stay informed about trends in fundraising and corporate giving. Now I don't read any of them. I only read Twitter. You should give it a try!

To get started, here are four fundraising experts and three hashtags on business giving to follow on Twitter.

People to follow:

1. **@JoeWaters (http://twitter.com/joewaters):** The name may look familiar because it's me! I've been active on
(*continued*)

(*continued*)
Twitter for several years now, and on average, tweet 15 to 20 times a day. I tweet a lot—but not exclusively—about fundraising with businesses. In the summer I tweet pictures of my flower gardens!

2. **@TweetCMF http://twitter.com/tweetcmf:** This is the Twitter handle for Cause Marketing Forum, the leader in information and education on nonprofit and business partnerships. The handle is managed by the organization's marketing director, Megan Strand. http://twitter.com/meganstrand

3. **@Cone (http://twitter.com/cone):** Boston-based Cone is a national leader in corporate social responsibility and cause marketing and has over three decades of experience in brand communications. I've learned a lot from Cone. So will you.

4. **@ForMomentum http://twitter.com/formomentum:** For Momentum is a leading cause marketing agency based in Atlanta. The team is very active on Twitter and other social networks.

Hashtags to follow:

- **#causemarketing:** Company and cause information and news, as well as many of my own tweets, are commonly tweeted with this hashtag.

- **#corpgiving:** This is another useful hashtag for following news on business giving.

- **#fwb40:** This is the hashtag for this book, *Fundraising with Businesses*. I'll be tweeting using this hashtag and following tweets that use it. If you have a question, comment, example, or success story to share, use this hashtag and see how hashtags make it easy to follow a topic!

STEAL THESE IDEAS!

1. Hashtag fundraisers are great, but why limit the fun to Twitter? Expand your fundraiser to include other hashtag friendly social networking sites: Facebook, Pinterest, Instagram, Tumblr, Pinterest, Google+, YouTube, and Twitter's Vine. Hashtags are the thing that links them all. See Figure 4.1. The more platforms you involve, the more people you'll involve and the more money you'll raise.

2. If you're planning a hashtag fundraiser for one of the more "visual" social networks (e.g. Youtube, Pinterest, Vine), remember to focus your campaign on the power of the image you're asking supporters to share. For example, a business partner may agree to donate $10 when attendees of your annual gala use the hashtag #GalaFun on Instagram, but the fun part is when people share their pictures from the event. Have fun with it! The hashtag is just a way of tracking the results.

3. Hashtags may be the future of business giving . . . if not business itself. Here's why. In early 2013, designer Donna Karan kicked off an innovative e-commerce campaign at New York Fashion Week. She sold a bracelet exclusively on Twitter to benefit Haiti. The bracelet is one of the first products available using Amex Sync, which lets you connect your Twitter account with your credit card for social shopping using hashtags. Once you've connected your account, you can tweet with the hashtag #BuyUrbanZenBracelet and look for an automated response from @AmexSync. The automated Twitter bot will @mention your Twitter handle with a link to confirm your purchase. If you tweet the confirmation hashtag within 15 minutes of the @AmexSync reply, your purchase will be complete. Pretty cool, huh? With a link between hashtags, our bank account and the things we love to buy, supporting a favorite cause may be just a hashtag away. Stay tuned!

FIGURE 4.1

Firehouse Subs Pickle Bucket Post-a-Thon Tapped Twitter, Pinterest, and Instagram

Source: Courtesy of Firehouse Subs.

4. Businesses that want a more direct link to sales before they give can use hashtags to track purchases. In a partnership between the Testicular Cancer Awareness Foundation (TCAF) and cake ball company, Sweet Ballz, whenever a person purchased Sweet Ballz at a 7-Eleven and posted it to Twitter or Instagram with the hashtag *#20kBallz*, Sweet Ballz donated $1 to the TCAF. The goal of the two organizations was to educate 20,000 men on testicular cancer. Remember, a two-step process to donate will mean less money for your non-profit. The business will get their proof of purchase, but it sacrifices donations.

FOR MORE INFORMATION

 You can see more examples of hashtag fundraisers by visiting http://fwb40.us/15jxg5i or scan the QR code to view them on your smartphone or tablet.

CHAPTER FIVE

Shopping Fundraiser

If you've ever shopped at a Macy's department store you've probably seen their *Shop for a Cause* fundraiser. To support non-profits, Macy's distributes savings passes for a one-day shopping event, which nonprofits can sell for $5 each. The nonprofit keeps the money and the donor can save 25 percent on purchases.

Macy's has raised nearly $50 million for nonprofits since 2006.

Selling savings passes is just one option for a shopping fund-raiser. You can sell tickets to a special event, such as a fashion or trunk show, or the business can donate a percentage or portion of sales for all purchases or just for specific purchases for an evening or forever!

Regardless of the type of shopping fundraiser you choose, your success hinges on one thing: your nonprofit's ability to motivate supporters to participate in the fundraiser. This is one type of business fundraiser in which the nonprofit will make or break the event.

MCDONALD'S HOSTS MCTEACHER'S NIGHT

To illustrate how a shopping fundraiser can happen at just about any business, take this example from Southern California's McDonald's restaurants and their McTeacher's Night.

To raise money for classroom supplies, field trips, and educational activities, teachers traded their classrooms for positions behind the McDonald's counter serving hungry diners.

Of course, students and their families turned out in force to see their teachers working under the Golden Arches. This was a great way to boost turnout for the event.

This one-day event involved 200 area schools and raised $140,000, a percentage of the total sales from the McTeacher's Night.

HOW IT WORKS IN 1-2-3

1. The business partner agrees to host a shopping event in its stores from which your nonprofit will receive a portion or percentage of the total sales from purchases that day.

2. The nonprofit and the business promote the fundraiser to their supporters and customers.

3. The day of the event, the business tracks purchases and donates a percentage of the total sales, or a portion of the sales from specific customers (e.g., shoppers who identify themselves as supporters of your nonprofit), to your nonprofit.

THINGS TO REMEMBER

*   Does your nonprofit have a large, active and loyal donor base that you can tap for a shopping fundraiser? The success of most shopping fundraisers hinges on the nonprofit's ability to drive supporters into the business. Although many businesses are happy to promote the event with their customers, they're banking that your involvement will bring in *new customers*— or at least some current customers for another visit.

How Businesses Choose a Nonprofit Partner

Businesses are waking up to the benefits of choosing a *good* charity partner. Not all nonprofits are created equal, and businesses are spending more time sifting through their choices to pick the right one.

(continued)

In order of importance, here's what they're looking for.

1. **A cause they love.** Businesses are populated with men and women who want to support a cause they care about. It can be kids with cancer, caretakers for the elderly, or saving the whales. When a business truly cares for a cause, it will put its heart and soul into a fundraiser. That makes all the difference.

2. **A nonprofit with an army.** Being passionate for a cause and supporting a nonprofit are not the same thing. You may have a passion for helping sick children, but which children's charity will you help? You have a lot of choices. Smart businesses pick nonprofits that have active, loyal supporters that will support a business fundraiser. There's a good reason why so many businesses are partners with nonprofits such as the Breast Cancer Research Foundation. The supporters of BCRF, and other cancer charities, are active and passionate consumers of pink products and services.

3. **A nonprofit that evokes emotion.** Human beings are drawn to emotional messages, especially when it comes to causes. Research shows that the top causes are women's causes followed by children, animals, and men (In this case, men are *behind* the dogs). It's no surprise that these are the causes businesses support most. If your nonprofit isn't in one of these groups, don't despair! You can and should lead with emotion. It may not be as powerful as children and puppies, but it pays to lead with the strongest emotional appeal you can muster.

4. **A nonprofit that fits with the business.** I call this "Garanimal fundraising." (Do you remember *Garanimals*? It's a line of kids' clothes that have animals on
(*continued*)

(continued)

their tags. A shirt with a giraffe tag goes with pants that have the same tag. But tags that have a horse on one and a giraffe on the other will make you look like a donkey. Go figure.). In fundraising partnerships, an equivalent of Garanimals occurs when a restaurant works with a food pantry—because it just fits. Or how about a construction company that works with a charity that builds homes, like Habitat for Humanity. There's nothing wrong with this approach, and it's how a lot of businesses choose a wonderful nonprofit partner. But love, loyalists, and emotion trump matchy-matchy.

A business that chooses a nonprofit solely on "match" reminds me of a scene from the Eddie Murphy movie *The Distinguished Gentleman*. Instead of writing his own speech, Murphy's character—a candidate for Congress—repeats a bunch of unrelated quotes from famous speeches that sound great but make no sense. In true movie fashion, Murphy's supporters clap wildly for him. Rest assured that such antics are only successful in the movies.

STEAL THESE IDEAS!

1. Turn your shopping fundraiser into a special event. A lot of stores will add a fashion or trunk show or recruit a local celebrity to boost attendance. Shopping fundraisers are called special events for a reason. They're supposed to be *special*—and not just another day of shopping that can be done anytime.

2. Encourage your business partner to sell pinups (see Chapter 15) a week or two prior to your fundraiser. You'll raise more money and target good prospects for the shopping event. Pinups are also a visible way for businesses to show how they

are giving back to the community. Several years back, I had success advertising a Halloween fundraiser by promoting it on a pinup. See Figure 5.1. Post event surveys revealed that one in five attendees learned about the event from the pinup.

3. Shopping fundraisers sometimes take the form of gift cards that retailers sell to nonprofits at a discount. The nonprofit then sells them to supporters at full price. It's not Macy's *Shop for a Cause*, but it's a start.

4. Organize a *cause mob*. A *cash mob* involves a group of people coming together to spend an agreed amount at a local business. It's a great way to encourage people to shop locally. But as UK corporate fundraising consultant John Thompson pointed out in *UK Fundraising* (www.fundraising.co.uk), a *cash mob* could be turned into a *cause mob* with people spending money at a business that has agreed to donate a portion to a good cause. A cause mob could also be part of a shop-walk (Chapter 21).

FIGURE 5.1

Pinups Can Raise Money and Promote Your Fundraiser

FOR MORE INFORMATION

 You can see more examples of shopping fundraisers by visiting http://fwb40.us/18iT1Vb or scan the QR code to view them on your smartphone or tablet.

CHAPTER SIX

Action-Triggered Fundraiser

When a consumer performs a specific action that triggers a contribution from a business to a nonprofit it's called an *action-triggered fundraiser (or donation)*. The consumer action can be just about anything: donating a coat, giving blood, test-driving a car, getting a flu shot, and so on. The choices are endless.

Action-triggered fundraisers are easy to set up and popular with consumers who have to act to give. Although these programs are criticized as "slactivism" because they ask for neither time nor money, when done well they leave the consumer, company, and cause smiling.

CHIPOTLE'S "BOORITO" SCARES UP FUNDS FOR FOUNDATION

Mexican grill Chipotle is a good example of a company that takes its customers' acts for charity seriously. Anyone who visits a Chipotle on Halloween *in costume* between 4 P.M. and closing gets their meal for just two bucks.

The money—up to a million dollars—goes to the Chipotle Cultivate Foundation, a nonprofit dedicated to sustainability and providing awareness about food-related issues.

A fun part of the 2012 *Boorito* fundraiser was a YouTube video of Frankenstein—aka Rob Riggle of *The Daily Show*—scaring people and knocking kids over as he professes his love for Halloween and the community.

HOW IT WORKS IN 1-2-3

1. Working with your business partner, identify what action will trigger the donation and how much you'll receive per action. As with most programs, it's smart to have a start and end date and to agree beforehand on a maximum donation.

2. Determine a way to track customer actions. Will you count the number of coats donated? The number of flu shots given? Or how many test-drives the car dealership had the weekend before President's Day.

3. At the end of the program, total the number of actions taken and collect your donation from your business partner!

THINGS TO REMEMBER

- Action-triggered fundraisers are sometimes a more difficult sell to businesses because, unlike other programs that collect donations from customers, the company is making the donation on behalf of the consumer. Naturally, businesses will ask, "What's in this for me?" A lot, actually. In the case of Chipotle, the program is a good opportunity to attract new customers who want to take advantage of the special offer. Also, costumed customers get their meal for two bucks, but they'll buy drinks, snacks, and so forth at full price. Stress the residual benefits to business owners and making a bigger pie for everyone.

- Digital action-triggered fundraisers are common and as successful as their offline counterpart. But they're not addressed in this chapter. Consult the chapters on Facebook (16), YouTube (39), Pinterest (7), for more details.

Five Nonprofit Lessons from Zombies

I'm a big fan of all-things zombie and especially the AMC television series *The Walking Dead*.

If you're not familiar with the show it's about a small group of men and women who must survive in a world turned upside down by a zombie apocalypse. Rick Grimes, a small-town police sheriff who's trying to protect his family and the stragglers they've picked up along the way, leads them.

Although you may not share my love for the semi-dead, you may agree with this: most of us are surrounded by these mute, will-less, dumb, sometimes evil, and dangerous brutes every day. The zombies stalking nonprofits are the people and situations they face daily that threaten their success or even their survival.

Scary stuff, for sure. Fortunately, my zombie-like interest in *The Walking Dead* has taught me a few lessons and tricks. Ignore them at your own risk!

1. Get In Shape

A lesson learned from *The Walking Dead* is that the weak, slow, or distracted quickly become zombie food. Your cause, too, will meet a horrible end if you're weak, outdated, or poorly conditioned.

How to stay alive: Make a commitment to something new that will make a real difference to your cause and stick with it. It could be updating your technology, learning social media or (my personal favorite) working with a business on a fund-raiser. The point is that you have to flex your muscles or someone else will have them for dinner.

2. Kill with Efficiency

The Walking Dead survivors have been on the run for some time. Not surprisingly, they've gotten good at using guns, knives, crossbows, metal poles, and anything else you could put through a zombie's brain (the only sure way to kill one).

(continued)

(*continued*)

Rick and his crew use what's at hand to get the job done. So should you.

How to stay alive: Take a good look at all the things your nonprofit does. What are your bread and butter programs that work year after year? Can you enhance their success or replicate another success from them? When the nonprofit I last worked for figured out the formula for raising money from businesses, we didn't stop, and we recruited 40 new corporate partners.

3. Beware of Small Spaces

People get eaten alive when they get trapped. It's a sad, gruesome way to die. And this could happen to you when you confine your nonprofit to one small area, whether it be grants, events, or individual and business donations. Limiting yourself to one thing will keep you cornered and vulnerable.

How to stay alive: Start exploring a direction for your nonprofit and set one new course before the end of the year.

4. You Need a Team

A lot of the characters on *The Walking Dead* don't like each other, but that doesn't stop them from sticking together. They know they're stronger together and wouldn't survive alone.

How to stay alive: Look around at your team. Are they people you can rely on or are they slowing you down and making you more vulnerable? Replace them with people who you trust and can help you survive.

5. Check the Back Seat

I can't tell you how many times someone has gotten eaten on *The Walking Dead* because they didn't look under a bed or in a closet or behind a door. Such a senseless way to go! But nonprofits, too, are sacrificing themselves for ridiculous reasons.

(*continued*)

How to stay alive: When it comes to fundraising with businesses, focus as much on your partner's success as your own. Know your assets and the value you bring to a partnership.

Being selfish is one sure way to unleash the zombies!

STEAL THESE IDEAS!

1. Action-triggered fundraisers can be incorporated into *any* business. Look at what the business does and build a consumer action around it. A coffee shop can donate money for every pound of coffee beans it uses. A restaurant can donate every time a member of the U.S. military dines there. A dentist can donate every time a patient turns in his Halloween candy, or posts a picture of his perfect smile on a bulletin board in the waiting room.

2. Action-triggered programs can involve anyone or anything. For example, dairy producer H. P. Hood offered to donate $200 for every home run, double play, and strikeout by the Boston Red Sox at Fenway Park. In Europe, Western Union agreed that every pass in the Europa soccer league, estimated at 80,000 every year, would trigger a day of education somewhere in the world funded by the financial services giant.

FOR MORE INFORMATION

 You can see more examples of action-triggered fundraisers by visiting http://fwb40.us/131TcnT or scan the QR code to view them on your smartphone or tablet.

CHAPTER SEVEN

Pin-to-Give Fundraiser

There's a simple reason why Pinterest has become a popular destination for business fundraisers with nonprofits: Pinterest is where all the people are!

After Facebook and Twitter, Pinterest is the third largest social networking site with tens of millions of users. This is impressive, considering that Pinterest launched just a few short years ago in March 2010.

Pinterest is a virtual pinboard where users can pin and organize the things they love. They can also share their pins with others.

In addition to being a top social networking site, Pinterest is a top destination for women, a key target audience for businesses as women do most of the household shopping. Research also shows that women, especially mothers, are strong believers in and supporters of companies that support social causes.

Pinterest has a large, growing audience of women who are fans of cause-conscious businesses. Why wouldn't you want to give a Pinterest fundraiser a try?

BEAUTY BRAND PINS TO GIVE CANCER SURVIVORS A BEAUTIFUL DAY

Beauty brand Elizabeth Arden is all about making women look their best. So is the nonprofit Look Good Feel Better, which teaches beauty techniques to cancer patients that have appearance-related side effects from their cancer treatments.

FIGURE 7.1

Elizabeth Arden's #PinItToGiveIt Board

Source: Courtesy of Elizabeth Arden.

Together, the two organizations created #PinItToGiveIt to donate 10,000 eyeliners to cancer survivors.

Elizabeth Arden created a board with a selection of relevant images and chose the hashtag #PinItToGiveIt. See Figure 7.1.

Next, Elizabeth Arden actively promoted the campaign on Pinterest and its other social networking sites. At the end of the campaign, Elizabeth Arden counted the number of repins at the bottom of each image and Look Good Feel Better collected its eyeliners. See Figure 7.2.

HOW IT WORKS IN 1-2-3

1. With your business partner, create a Pinterest board and decide what you want to be "pinned." Is it a standard image (Elizabeth Arden gave users several to choose from) or is any image acceptable so long as it includes a specific hashtag?

FIGURE 7.2

Look Good Feel Better Collected 579 Eyeliners from This Pin

Source: Courtesy of Elizabeth Arden.

Keep in mind, though, that your campaign needs a hashtag so you can track the results.

2. Decide how long the campaign will run and how much or what the business will donate each time the pin, with the accompanying image and hashtag, is repined.

3. At the end of the campaign, add up the number of repins and collect your donation.

THINGS TO REMEMBER

- Don't limit the promotion of your pin-to-give campaign to Pinterest. For all its growth and publicity, Pinterest isn't a standalone site. Your campaign will be more successful if you promote it on other social networking sites as well, especially Facebook.

- You can track your Pinterest campaign in a couple of ways. One way is the number of repins at the bottom of the original pin. See Figure 7.2. Another is to use the search bar on Pinterest (upper left on the website) and type in your hashtag (e.g., #PinItToGiveIt). As with Twitter hashtag fundraisers (see Chapter 4), it's important to use a unique hashtag so that search results will be limited to your campaign.

Pinterest Basics for Beginners

Compared to other social networks, Pinterest is the new kid on the block. I've been talking a lot about our new neighbor, but pardon my manners, not all of you have been introduced.

What is Pinterest?

It's a virtual pin board where "pinners" can organize and share the things they love, and find more great things from others. The most popular categories on Pinterest are Home, Arts and Crafts, and Style/Fashion.

What is a Pin?

A pin is an image or video. When you find something on the web you want to add to your boards, you can "pin it" to a board. The image links back to the site from where you got it.

What is a Board?

A board is where you categorize your pins. For example, as part of this book I've sorted my pins by chapters so you can explore other examples of the strategies I've discussed.

Scan the QR code or use the URL provided at the end of the chapter for more examples of pin-to-give fundraisers.

What is Repining?

When you see a pin you like on Pinterest you can repin it to one of your boards.

What is a Follower?

Like Facebook and Twitter, people can follow you on Pinterest, and you can follow them back. This means that you can see their pins and boards and they can see yours. They can also leave a comment on your pins.

STEAL THESE IDEAS!

1. Engage users by asking them to pin their own photos with a hashtag. For example, when customers at Firehouse Subs pin an image of their Firehouse Subs pickle bucket with #BucketsSaveLives Firehouse will donate $1 to the Firehouse Subs Public Safety Foundation.

2. Invest in a custom tab for your nonprofit's Facebook page so supporters can view Pinterest boards, follow, like, and repin all within Facebook, the biggest social networking site in the world. Let's face it, one of the best places to promote your Pinterest campaign is the place where supporters are spending even more time: Facebook.

FOR MORE INFORMATION

You can see more examples of pin-to-give fundraisers by visiting http://fwb40.us/1fuqcYn or scan the QR code to view them on your smartphone or tablet.

CHAPTER EIGHT

Text-to-Give Fundraiser

I have a love-hate relationship with SMS (short message service or text) and its fundraising counterpart text-to-give.

I love SMS because it's simple and everyone knows how to use it. There's also much to love about text-to-give, because it can be a fundraising superstar. Some nonprofits have raised tens of millions of dollars with text-to-give programs, particularly after disasters such as Hurricanes Katrina and Sandy, and the Haiti and Japan earthquakes.

I dislike text-to-give because after you take out the money it raises for disasters there's not much left to talk about.

So what's the verdict on text-to-give? Will your nonprofit be LOLing all the way to the bank or exclaiming WTH? That's what this chapter is all about.

THREE TEXT-TO-GIVE CAMPAIGNS TO LEARN FROM

So what's the best way for businesses and nonprofits to use text-to-give? Let's dial 411 and speak to three experienced operators who have successfully used text-to-give when disaster *hasn't struck*.

Tevolution

Tevolution, an iced tea beverage from Purpose Beverages, uses text-to-give to give back to good causes when customers input the codes found on every bottle. They also skirt the expense and hassle of text-to-give by using text to register the users' *wish to give*. Because the money comes from the company, they don't have to work with a third-party vendor to collect and process the dollars from consumers.

Global Poverty Project

Global Poverty Project uses text-to-give at its popular concerts in New York's Central Park. A captive audience and rock star appeals are a potent combination for text-to-give. You may not have Neil Young making you ask as Global Poverty Project did, but if you have a captive audience and a pitch from a local celebrity, it just might work.

Sporting events may also be a good place to try text-to-give. When Louisiana State University used a home football game to ask 90,000 football fans to text-to-give $5 to the United Way, over 2,500 fans responded and the campaign raised $8,500.

Mobile Loaves and Fishes

Mobile Loaves and Fishes teamed up with an outdoor media company to tell a powerful story of need that could be relieved by making a donation via text. The *I Am Here* campaign in Austin, Texas raised enough money to get a homeless couple, who were living beneath the billboard, into a home. See Figure 8.1. Was it a disastrous earthquake that prompted people to give? No. Did it shake people up enough to get them to give? You bet.

The lesson from all of these examples is that text-to-give is just a hammer. If you give people the right nail, they'll hit send.

HOW IT WORKS IN 1-2-3

1. You have to apply for a keyword and short code (e.g., Text the keyword "ALIVE" to the short code 90999). For more information you can visit the Mobile Giving Foundation's website www.mobilegiving.org.

2. Working with your business partner promote the keyword and short code everywhere (e.g., newsletters, register signs, billboards, store windows, labels, etc.).

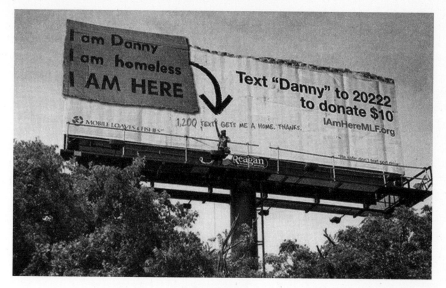

FIGURE 8.1

The *I Am Here* Text Campaign Raised Enough to Get a Homeless
Couple Off the Streets

Source: Courtesy of Mobile Loaves & Fishes.

3. The donation is charged to the donor's phone bill, collected
   by phone carriers, and distributed to your nonprofit.

THINGS TO REMEMBER

- Consider the audience you want to reach. Just about everyone
  uses SMS, but millennials (men and women born between
  1980 and 1999) are big users. If your business partner markets
  to this audience, SMS may be the tool for you.

- You'll need to choose a third-party vendor, such as mGive,
  which processes 85 percent of SMS donations, to execute your
  campaign. Text-to-give isn't something most nonprofits do
  in-house. A list of approved application service providers
  (APS) is available at the Mobile Giving Foundation website
  (www.mobilegiving.org).

- Giving options are limited. The most popular amounts are $5, $10 and sometimes $25. Currently, there are no recurring text donations.

- Make sure you understand the fees. Providers typically charge for setup, monthly usage, and per-message usage.

- If you can, add a website address or a QR code (see scan-to-give programs in Chapter 20) to your SMS fundraiser as another way for people to donate.

- Incorporate your keyword and short code in all your communication materials and share it with all your employees. It needs to be as well known and public as your nonprofit's website and phone number.

Four Ways to Close a Business Partnership

Congratulations! You've persuaded a decision maker to meet to discuss a fundraising partnership with your nonprofit. You're moving in the right direction. It's nearly impossible to close a partnership if you don't meet face to face with a decision maker.

But I bet you have nagging questions and doubts: "What do I do now? How do I turn this meeting into a partnership?"

Here's how not to leave the meeting empty-handed.

1. **Free is for me.** Most of the fundraising ideas in this book should be offered free of charge to the business owner. Asking the company to pick up the expenses for the program is an obstacle to closing the deal. I'm not suggesting you pay for all expenses. Rather, you need to invest in the program and you'll recoup your money (and a healthy profit) at the end the fundraiser. For example, pinups (Chapter 15) are generally inexpensive to produce—just a few cents for each one. But insisting that the business either pay or split
   (continued)

---

these expenses is just an obstacle to them saying *yes*, and to the riches that await you, the nonprofit, at the end of the program.

2. **Don't give them an excuse to say no.** Offer to handle all the work of the fundraiser, minus one important chore: anything that involves the business actually raising money for your organization. Being the work-horse behind the scenes (e.g., designing, printing, and shipping pinups or sourcing and ordering coin canisters) means the business can focus on raising money for your organization.

3. **Increase the number of touch points.** A strong business pitch from you is a good start, but get the business to tour your nonprofit so they can see the good work you're doing. Or ask an existing partner to recommend you by phone, meeting, or e-mail. The closer they feel to your mission, and the more positive feedback they get from supportive partners, the more likely they are to turn from prospect into partner.

4. **Be flexible and helpful.** Most of the time you won't leave the meeting with a new partner. If only life was that easy! Usually, it takes time and multiple meetings to close a deal. Avoid a flat-out no because it's difficult to overcome (A business owner explained the power of *no* to me early on in my career: "What part of *no* don't you understand?"). The second best answer after a *yes* is *maybe*. Agree to work with the business in any way possible, even if it's in a very small way. Focus on building rapport and goodwill. Keep them informed of other programs you're working on and share posts, articles, videos or presentations that relate to their business.

Remember: The best way to turn a prospect into a partner is to treat them as if they already are one.

STEAL THESE IDEAS!

1. Team up with a media partner. They have the promotional muscle to spread the word on your text-to-give fundraiser. Your goal with these TV, radio and outdoor advertising businesses is to get them to donate airtime or space so you can share a compelling story, image, or message to solicit text donations. Increasing awareness about your text-to-give campaign increases the chances that people will support it when they see it.

2. As we learned from the Global Poverty Project, teaming up with businesses that manage a large venue, such as a sports arena or entertainment venue, might be your best bet. Entertainers frequently solicit text donations from the stage. These stars do it with good reason: they have a captive, mobile audience that wants to please their idol. Sport arenas also have potential. The Washington Nationals major league baseball team has used its electronic scoreboard to ask fans to donate to the Children's National Medical Center in D.C.

3. It can take a long time to build a text subscriber list. If you tap a business that already has subscribers you won't have to wait. That's what St. Jude Children's Research Hospital did when they partnered with pizza delivery giant Dominos to ask patrons to donate $5 via text. Dominos was an early adopter in the mobile space and already had a large and active subscriber list.

4. You know what people love to get via text? Coupons! Work with a business partner to deliver a coupon to their subscribers, which, when redeemed, triggers a donation to your nonprofit.

5. SMS isn't just for fundraising. It's useful for engagement, cultivation, and action. To master its use, follow three text pros in the nonprofit world:
   ○ The World Wildlife Fund
   ○ Best Friends Animal Society

- National Geographic Society
- The Humane Society of the United States
- DoSomething.org.

You can start by joining their text lists. How good are these organizations? DoSomething.org alone has over 1 million text subscribers and has adopted a mobile-first strategy for communicating with supporters.

There's an old saying about not following a path and instead blazing your own trail. But when it comes to text, it's smart to follow a trail until you're ready to head off on your own.

FOR MORE INFORMATION

 You can see more examples of text-to-give fundraisers by visiting http://fwb40.us/17uQfxT or scan the QR code to view them on your smartphone or tablet.

CHAPTER NINE

Cash Donation

I'd wager that cash is probably the first thing that comes to mind when I say "fundraising with businesses." It's what every nonprofit wants from a business: *cold, hard cash*. It has a beautiful ring to it, doesn't it? Unfortunately, it's a siren's song that has led many a nonprofit to despair.

The problem is that cash donations from companies have been drying up for two decades. There have been blips of generous support, for sure. In the wake of disasters such as Hurricane Katrina, the Haiti earthquake, Superstorm Sandy, and the Boston Marathon bombings, companies donated tens of millions of dollars.

But according to Curt Weeden, a corporate-giving expert who oversaw Johnson & Johnson's philanthropy program and authored *Smart Giving Is Good Business*, America's private sector has cuts its charitable giving as a percentage of its profits *by half*.

A bright spot has been smaller businesses that employ one or more workers. They increased their giving during the Great Recession, but not enough to offset the decline in giving from some of America's biggest companies.

Whether you're targeting large or small companies, here's how to cash in.

UP-FRONT CASH MAY BE AN UP-AND-COMING TREND FOR BUSINESSES

The usual model for cash donations from businesses has nonprofits applying annually for support and then waiting, fingers-crossed, for a response. But, as first reported in *The Washington Post*, some companies are copying government grants and foundation givers and making multiyear pledges upfront.

One example is D.C. law firm Wilmer Hale, which has made a three-year commitment to Bread for the City. The nonprofit provides food, clothing, medical care, and legal and social services.

An up-front commitment is a win-win for both organizations. The company can coordinate resources in advance. It also gets to focus on one key area and watch the impact. The nonprofit gets to budget the money and can redirect its resources to other funding opportunities.

Successful businesses are skilled at exploiting a niche and investing in an opportunity. The next big area of growth for savvy businesses may be in their nonprofit partners.

HOW IT WORKS IN 1-2-3

1. Even small companies have guidelines for nonprofit gifts. Visit the company website or call them to get a copy.

2. Review the guidelines to determine if your nonprofit is a match. If it is, apply for a gift or follow the company's guidelines for submitting a request.

3. The guidelines should include information about when you can expect to hear back. If this date passes, give the company a gentle nudge via e-mail or phone, but not a minute before the date specified in the guidelines!

THINGS TO REMEMBER

- Go where you are loved. Don't waste everyone's time applying for money for which you're not qualified. If the company only supports schools and your nonprofit is a food pantry, don't bother. You're just clogging up the process and setting yourself up for disappointment. Also, quickly size up the company. Do they or do they not give cash to nonprofits? If they don't it's unlikely you'll be the first. Move on.

- Persuasion occurs through identification. Explain to the business how your nonprofit's mission fits with their goals. If you're calling on a local manufacturer and your nonprofit retrains people for the workforce, your request may resonate with the business.

- There are other ways to get cash from companies. Review my chapters on matching gifts (Chapter 29), dollars for doers (Chapter 36) and payroll deduction (Chapter 18). Some employers give their cash to employees to donate. Pomegranate juice maker, POM, gives each employee $2,000 to gift to causes of their own choice.

Thinkers, Feelers, Deferrers: The Three Types of Decision Makers

After nearly 20 years of talking to company decision makers, I've concluded that they can be put in one of the three buckets: thinkers, feelers, and deferrers.

Granted, no decision maker is ever just one type. I wish it was that simple! Most decision makers are combinations of the three. But one type tends to dominate. This is where you need to focus your pitch.

Thinkers. Facts and figures are the mainstay of thinkers. These folks pore over graphs figures and charts looking for value and return. The question you need to answer for them is "Does supporting your organization *make sense* for my business?"

Feelers. Emotion is the key to opening the feeler's heart, and their checkbook. They're motivated by your story because it tugs at their heartstrings. Supporting your organization just *feels right*.

Deferrers. Of the three types of decision makers, deferrers fascinate me the most because of their faith in others. If they see that ABC Company is involved with your nonprofit, then you can count them in, too. If Ms. Jones says it's a good idea to

(continued)

(*continued*)

support your organization, then it is! Deferrers aren't patsies, but credibility and reputation weigh more heavily in their decisions than they do for a thinker or feeler.

Sometimes the person they're deferring to is you. Deferrers want to work with people they admire, respect, and trust. As a nonprofit professional, it's not enough to be a courier. You have to be trustworthy, competent, professional, articulate, and polished.

You're a surrogate for the men and women who deferrers look to for guidance. A king's messenger doesn't just carry his seal. He, too, is well dressed and spoken. Be the king's man.

STEAL THESE IDEAS!

1. Giving professionals like Curt Weeden, who have spent lifetimes giving money to nonprofits, will tell you that cash donations are not the present or the future of business giving. You may need to quickly pivot to other types of giving. If the business owner doesn't donate cash, or if your organization's mission doesn't sync with the giving guidelines, perhaps they would donate product or services (see Chapter 10). If they have nothing in kind to donate, perhaps they have lots of stores and customers for pinups (see Chapter 15) or percentage of sales programs (see Chapter 1) or a large workforce you could tap for matching gifts (see Chapter 29). Look for the full scope of opportunity, and not just for the cash.

2. Look around your town or city at the nonprofits that *do* attract cash donations. What qualities do they share? First, they lead with strong emotional messages that attract gifts, especially over the holidays when cash is king. Your organization may not treat sick kids or save puppies from the pound, but every organization should lead with messages that pull at the (corporate) heartstrings. Second, these organizations, like yours, are making an impact in their chosen area, but here's

the difference. They're doing a good job *communicating the difference* they are making. Thanks to social media tools such as YouTube, Twitter, Facebook, Pinterest, Instagram, and blogs, nonprofits have an unprecedented ability to communicate their impact. But if you're still debating whether or not you should be on Facebook, you're wasting valuable time.

FOR MORE INFORMATION

 You can see more examples of cash donation programs by visiting http://fwb40.us/19co0mS or scan the QR code to view them on your smartphone or tablet.

CHAPTER TEN

Product Donation

Nonprofits want cash from businesses (see Chapter 9). But what they usually get is product. That's one of the conclusions you can draw from the donations of 105 companies that were tallied by *The Chronicle of Philanthropy*. Of the $12.1 billion donated by these businesses, only about one-third was cash.

There are two good reasons why businesses prefer to donate product instead of cash.

First, donating product has clear tax advantages. Companies can deduct up to two times the cost on their return. So, if a company donates $10,000 worth of disposable razors and it cost the company $1,000 to make them, they can deduct two times the cost or $2,000 on their corporate return. [I'm married to a tax accountant, but this isn't tax advice. Consult a tax professional for your specific situation.]

Second, product donations are tangible contributions that customers and investors—not to mention reporters and photographers—can *see*. If you paid attention to company support for Hurricane Sandy victims in 2012 you probably saw lots of company trucks delivering supplies and volunteers handing out branded products to the needy. In short, the leave behind impression of product donations is powerful public relations.

All this points to the likelihood that your next donation from a company will come in a box, not an envelope. Here's how to ensure that product is as welcomed as a check.

TELESCOPE MAKER HELPS KIDS SET COURSE FOR THE STARS

The value of a product donation is in the eye of the beholder. I used to run a large Halloween fundraiser in Boston. It was kind of a big deal. Annually, the event, dubbed *Halloween Town*, attracted 15,000 people.

Of course, you can't have a Halloween event without candy. So, for months beforehand we called candy makers across the country asking for product.

Much of what we received was perfect for the event, but some of it wasn't. We got candy that had passed its expiration date, or wasn't wrapped for distribution (Imagine getting a giant box full of chocolate malt balls!). It took time and money to dispose of this candy (I did most of the disposing. I must have gained 20 pounds!).

The lesson is that product donations are great, when they serve a useful purpose; when they don't, they can be a costly nuisance and 10 times more difficult to get rid of than they were to solicit in the first place.

One product donation program that hits the sweet spot is telescope maker Celestron's partnership with Astronomers Without Borders (AWB). AWB is committed to bringing astronomy to stargazers around the world, regardless of education or income. Celestron regularly donates some of its best telescopes, some of which sell for thousands of dollars, to Astronomers Without Borders.

But that's not all. Celestron has sourced a telescope for AWB and is warehousing and shipping the telescopes at no cost to the nonprofit.

You can own an AWB Telescope for just $199. According to Mike Simmons, President of AWB, "A significant portion of the profits will benefit AWB."

Together, Celestron and Astronomers Without Borders are bringing children together under the stars and reminding us all that "We all share the same sky." See Figure 10.1.

FIGURE 10.1

Astronomers Without Borders Is Bringing Stargazing to Developing Countries
Source: Courtesy of Astronomers Without Borders.

HOW IT WORKS IN 1-2-3

1. As with cash donations, companies often have guidelines for making product donations. Visit the company website or call them to obtain a copy.

2. Review the guidelines to determine if your nonprofit is the right match. If you are, apply for a product donation or follow the company's guidelines for submitting a request.

3. The company's guidelines should include information on when you will hear back. After this date passes, feel free to give the company a gentle nudge via e-mail or phone.

THINGS TO REMEMBER

- Go where you are loved. Don't waste everyone's time by applying for product donations that aren't a good match for your organization. If the company only donates school supplies and your nonprofit is a food pantry don't apply; there's no point in getting things just because you can get them. You're just clogging up the process and setting yourself up for disappointment. Also, size the company up quickly. Do they donate products or not? If they don't, it's unlikely you'll be the first organization they'll give product to. Move on.

- If the business doesn't have formal guidelines, you'll need to talk to someone at the company about their giving guidelines. Ask first if there is someone who handles this area. If not, inquire at the very highest level of the company, which is the president or owner. Always talk to people that have the power to make a decision independent of others.

- Persuasion occurs through identification. Explain to the business how your nonprofit's mission fits with their business mission. If you're calling on a local soup manufacturer and your nonprofit is a soup kitchen, your request may resonate with the business.

Four Ways to Turn Unwanted Gifts into Nonprofit Gold

Companies don't always donate products because of altruism. Sometimes there's a packaging change that makes a product obsolete. Or perhaps they made too many products. Or the product they thought would be a big hit and rushed to market is a big flop.

(continued)

Individuals have the same problems. They get an earlier version of Apple's smartphone, instead of the latest one. Sometimes they get more than one smartphone (granted, a good problem). Or they just get something they know they'll hate.

That's why nonprofits shouldn't limit their product donation requests to companies. They should inform their supporters of product needs and how they can turn an unwanted gift into nonprofit gold!

1. **Donate the unwanted gift.** If your nonprofit can't use the product, just about every town and city has an American Red Cross, Salvation Army, and Vietnam Veterans of America to donate clothes, electronics, kitchenware, and so on. If you're still stumped, check out TheGivingEffect.com. It lists over 1,000 charities that need everything from toys to art.

2. **Return the gift and donate the money to charity.** Over the holidays encourage supporters to return unwanted gifts and donate the cash to you. Remind them that you'll take store credits, too. Or give them a list of things you need to buy with their credit.

3. **Recycle the gift for charity.** If grandma's idea of giving you the latest technology is a Sony Walkman she picked up at a yard sale, recycle it with a nonprofit that can either give your electronics a good home or recycle it for profit. Thanks to a partnership between **Dell** and **Goodwill** and a program called Reconnect, you can drop off your electronics at one of 1,900 Goodwill locations across the United States.

4. **Stop the gift-giving madness before it happens!** Before the holidays or birthdays encourage supporters to give you a gift instead. Show them how you'll put their generosity to good use!

STEAL THESE IDEAS!

1. If a company won't give you product, maybe they'll sell it and give you the money instead. (See Chapter 11 for more information on company giveaways.) In its *Breadstick for Hunger Tour*, Italian food chain Fazoli's visited 22 cities handing out Fazoli's breadsticks to raise awareness and funds for Feed The Children. As a part of the tour, Fazoli's created a new flavor of Lemon Ice named *Giving Grape Lemon Ice* and donated $1 to Feed The Children for every one it sells throughout the summer.

2. If a company can't or won't donate a product maybe they can donate a piece or portion of it. For example, Detroit-based Empowerment Plan employs homeless women to make coats for the homeless that can also be used as sleeping bags. To support the effort, General Motors donated scrap sound-absorption material from its Chevy Malibu and Buick Verano models as insulation.

3. Is your nonprofit looking for a place to sell collected goods and services? Try the eBay Giving Works program. Once registered, your nonprofit can tap eBay's millions of users to sell items from which you'll receive 100 percent of the final sale price.

4. Curt Weeden, the author of *Smart Giving*, who I introduced you to in Chapter 9, has a great suggestion for nonprofits that want products donations from manufacturers: ask them to produce a bit more for the sole purpose of donating the product to you. As Curt explains in his book, this option sounds easier than it is, because it requires cooperation from many people within the company. Still, think about the benefits. If a bakery extends production for even a short time they'll produce extra inventory that can be shared with nonprofits—and put to a variety of uses. That's just what an organization in Boston, Community Servings, does before Thanksgiving each year. Knowing that restaurants, bakeries, and cafeterias are making pies for the holiday, Community Servings asks them to make pies for

them to sell in advance of the holidays. This annual event, *Pie in the Sky*, has been a huge success for this nonprofit that delivers nutritious, delicious meals to homebound patients with AIDS.

Curt has a good checklist for nonprofits before they ask for product donations:

☐ Do you really need the product donation? If you don't need it, don't ask for it.

☐ Evaluate any product donations for safety and quality standards. If the company wouldn't sell it on the open market, they shouldn't be giving it to you.

☐ Are there any potential PR ramifications for accepting a product donation? If your nonprofit is a food pantry and you get a truckload of junk food from a manufacturer, will you keep it? If you do, will the press criticize you for accepting it? Product donations are supposed to be a good thing, not food for a public relations disaster.

☐ Can you make a good case for why your nonprofit is a good destination for product donations? Do you have experience receiving, managing, and distributing product donations? Is that limited to within the United States, or are you experienced in foreign markets as well?

☐ Do you understand the tax incentives for product donations? Can you explain them to the company? If you can't, then you shouldn't be accepting products from them.

FOR MORE INFORMATION

 You can see more examples of product donations by visiting http://fwb40.us/1cBVX2m or scan the QR code to view them on your smartphone or tablet.

CHAPTER ELEVEN

Company Giveaway Fundraiser

Businesses have successfully used product giveaways for over a century. King Gillette, the founder of the Gillette safety razor, became a household name by giving away his razors to build demand for the blades.

Today, some of the biggest names in business use giveaways. Even Apple has given away certain models of its popular iPhone in return for a contract with a carrier. Apple also makes gobs of money from sales in its app store and on iTunes. Free is a gateway to getting paid.

Businesses are smart to use giveaways to create a consumer stampede. It's time that nonprofits worked with businesses to use free to raise money for their missions.

AD AGENCY GIVES AWAY SWEETS FOR GOOD

The Philadelphia based R&D unit of advertising agency allen & gerritsen is always experimenting with new technologies to discover how they and their clients can use them. They call it a&g Labs.

To find out if people would use their social media networks to talk about the company, a&g combined cause with chocolate and called it *Social Sweets*.

Packed with chocolate candy bars, the a&g team hit the streets of Philadelphia to give them away. See Figure 11.1. In return for the sweet treat, they asked people to say thank you on Facebook

FIGURE 11.1

a&g Hands Out Chocolate Bars for *Social Sweets*
Source: Courtesy of allen & gerritsen.

and Twitter. When they did, a&g donated a dollar to Philabundance, the region's largest food bank.

In just two hours, the Labs team gave away one thousand chocolate bars, which generated over 400 reactions on social networks. They gained some valuable insights into consumer behavior and donated $463 to the food bank.

Good works. So does giveaways.

HOW IT WORKS IN 1-2-3

1. Working with your business partner, pick an item to give away. Generally, the item has a connection with the business (e.g., pancakes from IHOP, cars from Toyota). However, this isn't a requirement (as ad firm a&g's choice of chocolate bars shows).

2. Determine who will be giving the item away, where, when, and for how long.

3. What will you ask in return for the giveaway? A vote? A donation? A tweet? Or nothing?

THINGS TO REMEMBER

- The key with any giveaway is choosing something that people want but that isn't expensive for the business to give away. That's probably one reason why International House of Pancakes (IHOP) gives away free pancakes on National Pancake Day. Compared to other items on the menu, pancakes are cheap to buy and make—and people love them! In return for giving diners free pancakes, IHOP asks customers to donate to the Children's Miracle Network (CMN). And they do. Since 2006, IHOP has raised over $10 million for CMN, which supports children's hospitals across the country.

- Just because you give something away doesn't mean it's free. Even free has a cost to it. We use YouTube for free but it's reported that the video service loses as much as $1 million a day. You have to carefully weigh what you're giving away and decide whether it's worth it or not. Giving away pancakes costs money, but IHOP has raised millions of dollars for a good cause and enhanced their reputation with diners, which may mean more pancake orders from paying customers. For IHOP, free has a cost, but it also has a return on investment. If it didn't they wouldn't have continued the giveaway for all these years.

- Company giveaways are different from promotions that give donors something *after* they donate. For example, Cold Stone Creamery has rewarded customers who make a donation to Make-A-Wish with a free ice cream. Company giveaways are different—no strings attached. IHOP customers can enjoy their free pancakes and choose not to donate. a&g gives away a chocolate bar and *asks* for a social share. The business and nonprofit are expecting generosity to be rewarded in kind. Happily, it usually is!

The Secret to Nonprofit Success

City Slickers was a popular 1991 movie that starred actors Billy Crystal and Jack Palance. If you remember the movie, you're probably feeling as old as I felt when I first recalled it.

There's a scene in the movie when Billy Crystal's character, Mitch, is alone with Curly, a surly, plain-talking cowboy that's teaching Mitch about cattle herding and life.

> *Curly*: Do you know what the secret of life is? [holds up one finger]
>
> *Mitch*: Your finger?
>
> *Curly*: One thing. Just one thing. You stick to that and the rest don't mean shit.
>
> *Mitch*: But, what is the one thing?
>
> *Curly*: That's what you have to find out.

Nonprofits need to take Curly's advice and focus on one thing. They need to shine one bright, piercing light on something. What the world needs is more lighthouses.

Even if your nonprofit is far from the ocean I bet you've seen one of these lighthouses of the nonprofit world. Pick three or four nonprofits you admire. They're most likely straddling some dangerous strait and directing their light to saving and protecting lives, easing suffering or delivering people from ignorance. One light.

They're focused on one thing and they do it well. Damn the rest.

The Ellie Fund, a small nonprofit in my hometown of Boston, is focusing its light on the challenges women face *living* with breast cancer. They support them with transportation to medical appointments, childcare, housekeeping, groceries, and meals.

(continued)

The Ellie Fund isn't searching for a cure for cancer. They don't give treatment advice. They don't help men or children, at least not directly. They only do one thing: they ease the difficult impact breast cancer has on women.

If only you were as steadfast, singular, and illuminating.

Stop diffusing your light by being too many things. Affix yourself to some hazard and be the beacon that saves someone from a terrible wreck. That's what nonprofit success is really about.

STEAL THESE IDEAS!

1. Company giveaways are a great way to raise money, but sometimes the public relations benefit can outweigh the cash. The National Literacy Trust in the United Kingdom partnered with McDonald's to distribute millions of books with Happy Meals. The Trust understood the opportunity the quick serve giant offered. In *Marketing Magazine* a representative said: "We are very supportive of McDonald's decision to give families access to popular books, as its size and scale will be a huge leap towards encouraging more families to read together." This was a great opportunity for the Trust to share its mission with McDonald's large customer base.

2. Giving away something expensive can work, too, but it's more difficult and riskier. First, it's more difficult to find a business that will donate an expensive product, such as a diamond ring or car. Second, because they can only give away one or two items, you'll need a raffle so people can buy a chance to win. This means more work for your nonprofit as the brunt of the tickets sales will fall on you. Still, expensive giveaways can work. Just double check to make sure you have a strong bench of volunteers and supporters and the sales skills to make the giveaway a success.

FOR MORE INFORMATION

 You can see more examples of company giveaway fundraisers by visiting http://fwb40.us/175DOYk or scan the QR code to view them on your smartphone or tablet.

CHAPTER TWELVE

New Hire Fundraiser

A major underpinning of this book is that just about everything a business does is a fundraising opportunity for a nonprofit. I'm not kidding. Some of these opportunities are obvious, such as asking shoppers for donations at the register, or getting employees involved in a charity road race. But others require resourcefulness and creativity.

Take the announcement of a new employee. It's a routine matter for most organizations. You put ad in the local business journal, send a letter to clients, or mention it in your newsletter.

However, for the cause-minded business and the alert nonprofit, it's another chance to support one another's goals.

COMPANY TURNS NEW HIRE INTO FUNDRAISING, OUTREACH OPPORTUNITY

When the U.S. division of shoe retailer FitFlop hired a new public relations manager for its New York office, they had three goals. First, to announce the hire to the media. Second, to gather some valuable intelligence to help the new manager do her job. Third, to help their fellow New Yorkers who had been displaced by Hurricane Sandy.

In the hiring announcement that FitFlop sent to the media, they asked recipients to share some fun details about themselves, either by returning the postcard or by e-mailing their new hire directly.

For each response, FitFlop offered to donate $15 to charities helping the victims of Hurricane Sandy.

HOW IT WORKS IN 1-2-3

1. Before you send out a new-hire announcement, pick a favorite cause to support.

2. Identify the action the recipient has to complete to trigger a donation. It can be a call or an e-mail, or, as in the case of FitFlop, returning a postcard. As always, it's smart to set a maximum donation.

3. Set an end date for the program and total the actions performed. Be sure to communicate the results to participants.

THINGS TO REMEMBER

- Make it easy for recipients to complete the action that will trigger the donation. If you make it too complicated, people won't do it.

- Be sure to set an end date to encourage recipients to act now.

Three Ways to Become a Trusted Fundraising Advisor

Real success in fundraising happens when you become a *trusted advisor*, a person who is sought out for his or her advice and guidance.

I knew I had arrived as a trusted advisor when companies started calling me between fundraising programs for all sorts of social media and fundraising advice.

I was happy to help.

Being a trusted advisor solidified and grew my relationship with these companies and led to new opportunities. It also helped me weather the recession better than others who weren't as trusted.

Becoming a nonprofit consigliore doesn't happen overnight. It requires *character, competence, and confidence*. Here's how you can master the three C's of credibility.

(continued)

Character

To be trusted you have to be trustworthy. For me, this meant being honest with people about what I was trying to accomplish, how it worked and what I expected them to do. Showing your business partner that character is more than just a word is what puts the "trust" in *trusted advisor*.

Competence

In addition to being trustworthy, you need to be competent. You need to know what you're talking about. It's not enough for you to read this book and my blog. You need to apply what you've learned to your nonprofit and its business partnerships.

Confidence

You have to be able to communicate your character and competence. A trusted advisor is poised, professional and knows how to play his or her part. They dress, act, and speak in a way that demonstrates their confidence and reflects the confidence that people have in them.

STEAL THESE IDEAS!

1. A hiring announcement is just one option. Employee promotions and new product launches (see Chapter 34) are other opportunities to link an announcement to a donation.

2. Let the new hire choose the nonprofit to support. People want to work for a company that cares and gives back to the community. This is a great chance for a company to make a *good* first impression with employees and customers.

FOR MORE INFORMATION

A new hire fundraiser is a niche strategy so there's no accompanying Pinterest board. I suggest you scan the QR code at the end of Chapter 34 on launch fundraisers for more examples of fundraising with new ventures.

CHAPTER THIRTEEN

Cause Product Fundraiser

It's easy to confuse a cause-related product with a cause product. But as Mark Twain said, "The difference between the right word and the almost right word is the difference between lightning and the lightning bug!"

A cause-related product is an ordinary product that business temporarily use to support a cause. For example, when you buy a Dairy Queen *Blizzard* on *Miracle Treat Day*, DQ will donate the proceeds to the Children's Miracle Network. The day after Treat Day they'll still be selling Blizzards—thank goodness!—but not to benefit a cause.

On the other hand, a cause product is made specifically to benefit a cause. For example, Absolut has created a line of "city" vodkas that benefit causes in their namesake city. Absolut Boston benefited the Charles River Conservancy, an environmental group that protects Boston's historic river. The first city vodka, Absolut New Orleans, raised $2 million for the victims of Hurricane Katrina. The product is the cause.

The good news is that to launch a cause product you don't need the backing of a big company or the urgency of a disaster, but you will need to think bigger than usual, and prepare for some bumps, if they strike.

BEER FOR A CAUSE AIDS FAMILY OF FALLEN FIREFIGHTER

For Watch City Brewing Company's owner Jocelyn Hughes and brewers Aaron Mateychuk and Kelly McKnight, it all started with a desire to help a family that had lost its husband, father, and provider in a terrible fire.

It was December 8, 2011, when firefighter Jon Davies ran into a burning building in Worcester, Massachusetts to search for a missing tenant. He never came out.

Jon left behind a fiancée and three sons. Brewer Aaron Mateychuk's brother, Jamie, a member of the Worcester Fire Department, wanted to help Davies' family, and Aaron offered to help. Together with Jocelyn and Kelly, the Waltham, Massachusetts, based pub brewed *Rescue One Kölsch* to honor Davies and raise money for his family. See Figure 13.1.

To date, the German-style golden ale named after Worcester's Rescue One Fire Company has raised $3,000 for Davies' family. It's raised thousands more as supportive firefighters from across New England have purchased the beer in bottles and kegs and auctioned them off at local firefighter events.

The response has been tremendous. "We've brewed and brewed and brewed," said brewer Kelly McKnight to Boston's local Fox News affiliate. "We can't keep up with the demand."

FIGURE 13.1

Rescue One Kölsch

Source: Courtesy of Watch City Brewery.

Rescue One Kölsch isn't the pub's first beer for a cause. In 2004, they worked with Red Sox pitcher Curt Schilling on an ale to fight ALS. Watch City has even brewed ale to help the Bermuda Family Centre. "There's more poverty on the island than people realize," said Hughes. "We responded to where the need was."

For Watch City Brewing Company, the priority is making a difference first, but the benefits of selling *Rescue One Kölsch* are clear. They've sold a lot of beer and a distributor has already approached them about expanding their business. At the very least, Watch City has earned a few karma points.

HOW IT WORKS IN 1-2-3

1. Working with your business partner, identify a cause product to support your cause. As always, determine how much will benefit your cause, the minimum and maximum donation and the start and end dates of the program.

2. Develop the offering, the packaging, and the marketing that will support the campaign. The nonprofit and the business promote the fundraiser to their supporters and customers.

3. When can you expect to receive donations from the business? Monthly? Quarterly? Or at the end of the program?

THINGS TO REMEMBER

- Creating a cause product to benefit your cause may require a lot of time and effort. That's why you should ask for a minimum commitment of support from the business owner. This amount will vary depending on the business and the product. For example, Pandora Jewelry produces a special pendant, among other items, that benefits Komen for the Cure. Komen receives 5 percent of the retail sales price per item. But the breast cancer charity is guaranteed to receive a minimum of $1 million. So if the pendant doesn't sell, for whatever reason, Komen is still $1 million richer for the effort.

- Cause products feature your nonprofit, so make sure it's a promotion you can be proud of. Not long ago, a gun maker produced a "pink" pistol to increase awareness of and support for breast cancer causes. Cancer causes moved quickly to distance themselves from a cause product that would surely backfire.

- Transparency should be a key feature of your cause product. See Chapter 1 for five best practices. David Hessekiel, founder and president of Cause Marketing Forum, and one of the most respected names in the field, summarizes the recommendations: "Remember to *concisely and specifically* communicate the impact of that consumer action or donation in your cause messaging. Insist that your partners do the same."

- Cause products have a longer shelf life than many of the other fundraisers discussed in this book. Pinups (see Chapter 15), for example, are generally sold for two to four weeks. However, a cause product can sell for months or even years. Make sure you're clear on the start and end dates of the program and that both partners are committed to the long haul.

The Best Business Partner Is the One You Already Have

Every nonprofit wants to recruit new business partners, but your best bet to raise more money is to find new ways to work with your existing partners. It just might lead to a new partner.

Here's how to turn an existing partner into a better partner.

Be Insanely Helpful

Don't take a one-and-done approach with partners. Share new ideas with them. Follow, like, comment, and share their updates on social networks. Brag about them to everyone you

(continued)

meet. Be a real partner, which means you are focused on their interests even when they're not raising money for you.

Target New People

Make a new friend in the company that isn't in community relations or the company foundation. The folks in marketing have larger budgets but need bigger ideas if you hope to woo them. Human resources will listen, but only if you can help meet their challenge of engaging employees.

Master Useful Skills

Because many companies are still struggling with social media, position yourself as an expert that can help them in multiple areas. That means you need to be an expert on blogging, Twitter, Facebook, Pinterest and so forth. It also means you need to be up to speed on things like mobile technology and marketing to Millennials, the next generation of consumers.

Play Leapfrog

Your current partners are your best sources of referrals to new partners. Ask them to introduce you to their business contacts. Having one business partner may be your best chance to recruit another.

STEAL THESE IDEAS!

1. To save time and money, a cause product can be an existing product that's renamed to support a cause. For example, for two months in 2012, Turkey Hill Ice Cream renamed its Fudge Ripple ice cream *Four Diamonds Fudge* in honor of the Four Diamonds Fund. Based within Penn State Hershey Children's Hospital, the Fund provides financial and emotional support for pediatric cancer patients and their families. Turkey Hill donated a portion of the proceeds from each sale to the fund. Think of the possibilities at restaurants, bakeries, and coffee shops. A favorite entrée,

cupcake, or drink can be renamed for a limited time to support your cause!

2. A limited-edition-cause product can also drive donations. In the aftermath of the Boston Marathon bombing, running shoe maker New Balance scoured its warehouse for the remaining 890v30 BOSTON edition running shoe and sold the remaining 202 pairs on a first-come, first-serve basis. All monies raised supported the victims of the bombing.

3. Cause product partnerships with small businesses can hinge on the nonprofit's ability to drive sales. Watch City Brewery learned after the fact that firefighters were perfect customers for Rescue One because they belong to a large, fraternal group. Firefighters bought Rescue One, and shared it with other fire departments and with family and friends. Watch City learned from the experience and is considering brewing a special beer to support animal causes. They believe that this community is equally passionate and puts their money where their hearts are. Does your cause have a dedicated group of loyalists? Can you move them to buy? This should be a key focus of your cause product pitch.

FOR MORE INFORMATION

 You can see more examples of cause product fundraisers by visiting http://fwb40.us/13djXWy or scan the QR code to view them on your smartphone or tablet.

CHAPTER FOURTEEN

Office Pool Fundraiser

People love March Madness, the yearly NCAA college basketball tournament, so much that they drop everything to fill out brackets, watch the games and track the results. This is especially true at work as employees are following the day games and forming office pools with their colleagues.

Some companies have adopted an "If you can't beat them, join them" attitude by taking the lead in forming office parties and giving employees time off to enjoy the *madness*.

But savvy businesses and nonprofits that understand that passion is the key driver of purpose are treating March Madness as a *good thing* and using the tournament to raise money for causes.

HOW ONE EMPLOYEE BUSTED HIS BRACKET FOR CANCER

Justin Goldsborough hates cancer.

A colleague of his has an 18-month old who's undergoing a second round of chemotherapy. One of his best friends from high school lost his dad to lymphoma. Another friend lost his mom just a few weeks after doctors told her she was in remission.

Justin has had enough of cancer. But instead of putting a stake in the ground against the disease, he dribbled past it with a March Madness bracket challenge for his colleagues and friends in Kansas City.

Justin raised over $2,000 for the Leukemia & Lymphoma Society of Kansas City. You can do the same for your favorite organization.

1. Visit ESPN's Tournament Challenge to start a group

ESPN.com makes it easy to start or join a bracket challenge. It takes just a few minutes to fill out your bracket and then compete against friends, family, and other fans. "You just fill out your brackets and they take care of the rest," said Justin. You can see which teams have won and lost and who in your group has bragging rights.

He suggested a $25 donation to join his bracket challenge.

Justin is quick to point out that you don't have to use ESPN. Most of the other big-name sports websites—CBS, *Sports Illustrated*—have bracket games. Or you can do it the old-fashioned way with pen and paper.

2. Set up an event page on Facebook

Create a Facebook event page for your challenge so you can connect with all your family and friends on the biggest social network. Justin's Facebook event page included a link to his ESPN group page and another link to his donation page.

3. Set up a donation page

Justin used a donation page provided by the Leukemia & Lymphoma Society, which makes sense, since he's active with the nonprofit. However, if you're supporting a different charity you can create your own fundraising page right at Razoo.com, or another fundraising site.

Be sure to include a link to your donation page on your Facebook event page, and vice versa.

4. Promote the challenge through your other networks

Facebook is a great place to promote your bracket challenge, but don't forget e-mail and other social networks such as Twitter. Use everything you have to get the word out.

Justin suggests adding some prizes to sweeten the pot. "March Madness is about having fun competing against one another," he said. "Anything you can do to enhance that excitement will just make the challenge better."

Many of the people in Justin's group are colleagues of his from the Kansas City public relations community. Although his March Madness pool isn't company sponsored, management is supportive of his *office pool for a purpose.*

"Having a regular office pool and a pool for charity are seen very differently," he said. "Doing a pool for charity just sits better with the boss. It helps a lot that she and just about everyone else in the office are big fans of the tournament."

HOW IT WORKS IN 1-2-3

1. Employees create brackets of which teams they think will win every game, including the NCAA Basketball Championship game.

2. To include their bracket in the office pool to compete for bragging rights, employees have to make a donation to the nonprofit the company has selected to receive the funds.

3. The funds raised are donated to a nonprofit.

THINGS TO REMEMBER

- Let's be clear: March Madness office pools, or any workplace betting for that matter, are illegal in most states. Nonprofits should consult with their state's attorney general's office about workplace betting before proceeding. Nonprofits and companies should know the law, even if they plan to break it. Keep in mind that an official pool for a cause may help "sanitize" an office pool and make it more acceptable (still illegal, but acceptable). After recommending that betters keep the stakes low, legal experts say that involving a cause may make an office pool a safer bet.

- Nonprofits should target companies that are already committed fans of the tournament. These companies are comfortable with the legal conundrum of workplace betting. They also know firsthand just how consuming and addictive March Madness can be for employees. According to a study from outplacement firm Challenger, Gray & Christmas, the tournament costs U.S. businesses $134 million in lost wages in 2013. In short, March Madness is like a party, and you don't want your nonprofit blamed if employees enjoy it too much.

- Give employees that don't follow March Madness, or approve of betting the workplace, another option to donate, such as a dress-down day (see Chapter 24) that coincides with the dates of the tournament.

Machiavelli's Guide to Fundraising with Businesses

Niccolo Machiavelli, the Italian diplomat who wrote the classical treatise *The Prince* 500 years ago, probably would have been a big fan of for-profit and nonprofit partnerships. For a man so interested in statecraft, Machiavelli would appreciate the bottom-line benefits to causes and companies.

Some have called Machiavelli a manipulator. I see him more as a realist. He was practical and committed to getting things done in any way possible.

That doesn't mean Machiavelli didn't believe in ethics, morals, and scruples. He did, but not just because doing good was the right thing. It was frequently the best thing for any savvy prince to get what he wanted.

Although Machiavelli never participated in an office pool for charity or "liked" a Facebook page to trigger a donation, his advice transcends the renaissance and politics. It can inform us in our efforts to woo a new prince: consumer attention, favor, and their almighty dollar.

"Everyone sees what you appear to be, few really know what you are."

Cause-related promotions and fundraisers are about marketing and perception, not truth and reality. Smart causes lead with their strongest emotional appeal to engage consumers quickly and powerfully. Other nonprofits worry that this one appeal is limiting and won't accurately reflect its full mission. You'll have plenty of time to explain and expand on your work after you set an emotional hook.

(continued)

"Men are driven by two principal impulses, either by love or by fear."

The emotional appeal for fundraising has to tap something that consumers either deeply love (e.g., pets, green spaces, children) or seriously fear (e.g., cancer, polluted environment). Whether it's love or fear, your appeal should elicit a strong response from consumers.

"Hence it comes that all armed prophets have been victorious, and all unarmed prophets have been destroyed. . . . Before all else, be armed."

Are you truly ready to try fundraising with businesses, which demands staff, time, money, and a strong back to row upstream? Fundraising with businesses is much easier when you have a partner already lined up. But what if you don't? Are you skilled enough to sell a prospective business on the fundraiser? Do you know how working with a nonprofit can give businesses a competitive edge that goes beyond product and price? Arm yourself for success. Or be prepared to fail.

"Where the willingness is great, the difficulties cannot be great."

Nothing is accomplished without enthusiasm. If you're excited about and committed to fundraising with businesses you'll overcome any hurdle, meet any challenge. But if you're just going through the motions because your boss told you to, expect half-hearted results to match your half-hearted efforts. Machiavelli said that nothing is accomplished without danger. But no danger was ever surmounted without a strong will to succeed.

"The vulgar crowd always is taken by appearances, and the world consists chiefly of the vulgar."

Try to view your fundraiser through the eyes of ordinary consumers and supporters that may be learning about it for the first time. How do you think shoppers felt when they

(continued)

(*continued*)
discovered that a special tee shirt created to support National Public Radio wasn't really benefiting NPR?

Both NPR and Urban Outfitters sold the tee shirt on their respective web sites. But, unbeknownst to many consumers, purchases at Urban Outfitters didn't trigger a donation. Only purchases made on the NPR site triggered a gift. Naturally, people were upset because this wasn't explained on the retailer's website. Seeing is believing, and people want to see the fine print.

For Machiavelli, success depended on a prince's ability to prepare for the future and execute his designs without fear, hesitation or regret. If you add transparency, honesty, and authenticity you'll avoid becoming the cunning, grasping Machiavellian that *The Prince* sought to overthrow.

STEAL THESE IDEAS!

1. Sweeten the pot by asking employees to donate to your nonprofit each time they bust or beat their bracket. You'll raise more money. Your nonprofit can reward winning employees with tees, sweets, or gift cards.

2. Use the interest and excitement around March Madness to launch a related fundraiser. For example, Gold's Gym hosts *March Music Madness* and encourages members to pick their favorite workout songs. Like the tournament, it begins with 64 songs, before cutting down to 32, and then the "Sweet 16," "Elite 8," "Final 4" and, of course, the championship. Each song is associated with a charity, which receives $5,000 if they win the championship.

3. Don't limit office pools to the NCAA Basketball Tournament. Find out what employees are passionate about and create a charity office pool for it. It can be for the Oscars, the NFL Playoffs, *American Idol*, or *Downton Abbey*! Maybe it's a dead pool for which character will exit *The Walking Dead* or *Game of*

Thrones. They all work the same way as a March Madness office pool. To participate, employees have to make a donation to your nonprofit.

FOR MORE INFORMATION

 You can see more examples of office pool fundraisers by visiting http://fwb40.us/14Y9aRa or scan the QR code to view them on your smartphone or tablet.

CHAPTER FIFTEEN

Pinup Fundraiser

Paul R. Jones, the blogger behind the popular business fundraising website CauseMarketing.biz, introduced his readers to paper icons in a 2007 post.

> What are paper icons? They're slips of paper emblematic of a cause typically placed next to a cash register and sold as impulse items.
>
> They're relatively cheap to produce, even in small print runs. In large runs they might be less than a penny apiece.
>
> In North America the typical sales price is $1, although larger dollar amounts have been tried. After the icon is purchased, it's common to write the name of the purchaser on the icon. During the promotional period, the icons are displayed in the window, along a wall, strung above the cash registers, etc.

Paul knows what he's talking about. As a former fundraiser for Children's Miracle Network, he helped raise tens of millions of dollars with paper icons.

Paul dislikes the term *paper icons*. So do I. That's why I call them *pinups*. Others call them mobiles, paper plaques, and scannables.

We can debate the name, but what you can't argue with is the success of pinups as a fundraiser with businesses. "Done right, they are a license to print donations," said Paul.

Children's Miracle Network and their signature paper balloons are just one pinup success story. St. Jude Children's Research Hospital, Muscular Dystrophy Association and Make-A-Wish have raised tens of millions with pinups. In early 2013, the Muscular Dystrophy Association and Lowe's Home Improvement raised $8.8 million with Shamrocks, MDA's well-known pinup program. This was $1 million more than the previous year.

Even a local pinup program can break six figures.

Along with percentage of sales programs (see Chapter 1), pinups are one of the most lucrative fundraisers you can launch with a business.

Put a pin in this chapter. It could raise a lot of money for your nonprofit.

SHARE OUR STRENGTH AND SHAKE SHACK USE PINUPS TO FIGHT HUNGER

Working together, large nonprofits and businesses can raise millions of dollars with pinups. But that doesn't exclude smaller charities and businesses from working together.

A great example of a midsize partnership is *The Great American Shake Sale* launched by Shake Shack and Share Our Strength. Over a few weeks in 2012, this modern roadside burger stand blew through its original goal of $25,000 and raised over $135,000 with pinups. See Figure 15.1.

But what's really impressive is that Shake Shack raised six figures from just nine participating stores. One location in New York City raised over $28,000.

Shake Shack's success wasn't a fluke. In 2013, they raised a whopping $285,000 for Share Our Strength.

Here's how they did it.

They Laid the Groundwork

It started in 2011 when Share Our Strength's founder and CEO, Billy Shore, spoke to the Shake Shack senior management team about *No Kid Hungry*, the nonprofit's program to end childhood hunger.

"It lit a fire for giving and inspired us to create *The Great American Shake Sale*," said Randy Garutti, Shake Shack's CEO.

They Trained Employees

With the help of Share Our Strength, Shake Shack trained its staff to educate guests about the issue of childhood hunger. Moreover, it made the register ask a company priority. Every employee was trained to ask: "Would you like to donate two dollars to end childhood hunger?"

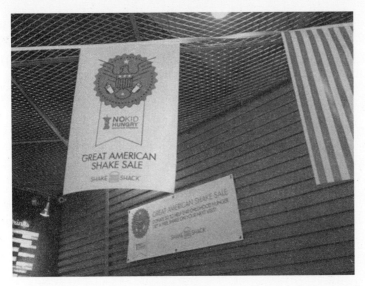

FIGURE 15.1

Shake Shack's Pinup for *The Great American Shake Sale*
Source: Courtesy of Share Our Strength.

They had Fun

According to Emily Kokernak, a nonprofit executive and regular at Shake Shack's Battery Park location in New York City, the store had a party-like atmosphere. "They were just having fun with the program," said Emily.

They Incentivized Customers

Shake Shack gave customers a powerful reason to donate. For every $2 donation, Shake Shack gave the donor a $5 coupon for a free shake. I know firsthand that customer incentives work since I've used them in my own pinup programs.

Pinups are an easy and lucrative fundraiser with businesses. But like every effort, plenty of advance planning is needed. Education, training and incentives are the keys to pinup success.

HOW IT WORKS IN 1-2-3

1. Working with your business partner, design, print, and ship the pinups.

2. At checkout, cashiers ask customers if they want to donate—usually a dollar or two.

3. The cashier collects the money and the consumer signs her name to the pinup, which is then displayed in the store.

THINGS TO REMEMBER

- Always work with the businesses' point-of-sale system to process donations. For more details read "Four Ways to Track Donations from Register Fundraisers" in Chapter 2.

- The cashier's "ask" is crucial to your success. Even when asked, not all customers will give. But if you don't ask, no one will give.

- Since the ask is key, don't spend a lot of money on making fancy pinups, posters, register signs, banners or buttons. These so-called *promotional items* just give cashiers a reason *not* to ask the customer to give. "The customer is being told to give everywhere they look," the cashier will rationalize. "I don't need to ask them." This sounds reasonable, but you now know better.

Pinups 101

Point-of-sale programs—pinups AND register programs (Chapter 2), roundups (Chapter 30), donation boxes (Chapter 3)—raise the majority of consumer donations each year. A 2013 study from the Cause Marketing Forum showed that 63 point-of-sale programs raised $358 million in 2012 alone!

However, the dominating point-of-sale tactic is pinups. People ask me all the time, "What is a pinup?"

1. A pinup (see Figure 15.2), which is sometimes called a paper plaque, paper icon, scannable, or mobile, is sold in restaurants, department stores, and any other place that has customers and a register.

(continued)

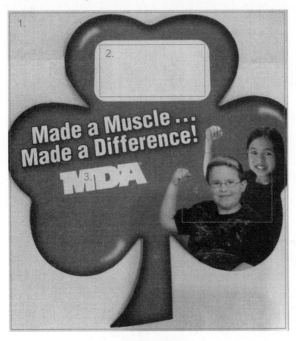

FIGURE 15.2

Front Side of Pinup

Most pinups are sold for between $1 and $5, although I've seen them sold for more and less. When the customer buys one, the donation is added to their bill. They usually sign their name to the pinup, which is then displayed somewhere in the business to show customer support of the program.

Most pinups aren't that big, just several inches tall and wide. They can be any shape, or die cut to look like a teddy bear, shamrock, heart, and so on. The paper used for pinups is usually inexpensive, and for good reason as just about all pinups will end up in the trash at the end of a program.

(*continued*)

(*continued*)

Most pinups cost anywhere from a few cents to a dime apiece to produce. The most I ever paid for a pinup was 18 cents each, but it was die-cut, four-color, large, perforated, and so on. Yours will probably be cheaper. As always, it depends on your designer, printer, shipper, and your willingness to shop around and negotiate.

2. Most pinups have a spot on the front where the donor can write his name. It's not necessary, but it does make the pinup a bit more personal.

3. Most pinups have the nonprofit's logo on the front with some kind of tagline.

4. Putting a picture on a pinup is a good idea because it puts a face on the campaign. You're not just giving to a charity when you buy the pinup in Figure 15.2. You're helping those kids!

5. The back of a pinup includes a barcode that can be scanned at the register. This makes it easy for cashiers to process the donation and for the business to track and report the donation to the nonprofit. When I began my career in the nonprofit world in the 1990s, cashiers used to keep donations in an envelope next to the register. It's not the safest way to handle donations. If a business won't or can't use a barcode (e.g., bakery, coffee shop) a good option is to designate a button or purchase code on the register to record the donation.

6. The back of the pinup usually includes additional information on the nonprofit, like its mission statement.

7. The shamrock pinup from MDA is a classic design that hasn't changed much in the past four decades. Yeah, it's been around that long. See Figure 15.3. Other options for the pinup include coupons, which means printing a larger pinup. However, coupons are a worthwhile investment as they incentivize shoppers to give.

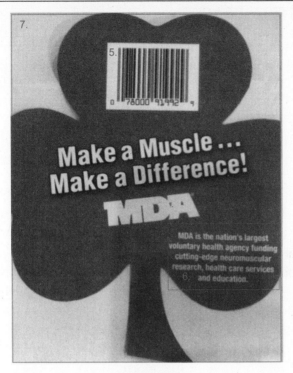

FIGURE 15.3

Back Side of Pinup

Businesses also like coupons, especially when other business partners in the program are distributing them to potential new customers. Nonprofits don't realize that pinups are a great place to promote a program or an upcoming event (e.g. charity bike ride, walk or run). It sure beats paying for advertising.

Some consumers may find charity asks at the register annoying, but they also tend to give more money and more frequently when a cashier makes the ask. Not everyone will love you, but you will love the results.

Virtual pinup programs are also an option. Several companies that are raising money with online fundraising programs are described in the following section.

STEAL THESE IDEAS!

1. Want to raise a lot of money with pinups? Target businesses that have lots of locations and foot traffic. The usual suspects are restaurants, supermarkets and department stores. But also visit coffee shops, fast lube businesses, gas stations, and even the cafeterias within large companies.

2. Don't be afraid to think outside the pinup. Depending on the business, you may not need a pinup at all. Displaying the donation request on a credit card terminal is becoming increasingly popular. A register promotion at BP Gas Stations in 2012 in support of four local Paralympic Sport Clubs in New York and New Jersey involved a window cling instead of a pinup.

3. If your current charity event (run, walk, ride, gala, etc.) has sponsors, convert them to pinup partnerships. Remember, when it comes to businesses that have a lot of locations and customer foot traffic, you'll almost always raise more money from customers than you will from the company checkbook.

4. Turn the program into a contest for cashiers and stores. When Tractor Supply Company (TSC) hosted its annual Paper Clover Fundraiser for youth organization 4-H, TSC kept an online leaderboard to keep the pressure on associates. In 2012, TSC raised nearly $500,000 for 4-H.

5. Take your pinup program online! Does your business partner have a busy e-commerce site? Ask them to solicit donations at checkout. Supporting good causes is a common practice in the 400 Build-A-Bear Workshop stores around the world. But consumers can also support their *Beary Big Heart* program when they buy online at BuildABear.com. Shoppers can donate a dollar to the Children's Heart Foundation at checkout. See Figure 15.4. If your business partner is looking for a nontechnical solution for their site, you should visit Charitablecheckout.com. They offer a free widget that makes the process simple for your partner and lucrative for your nonprofit!

Donate Today!!

Would you like to donate $1 to support the Children's Heart Foundation? Please click add to basket to donate today!

ADD TO BASKET   Donation - $1.00

The Children's Heart Foundation

FIGURE 15.4

This Retailer's Website Allows You to Donate a Dollar at Checkout

FOR MORE INFORMATION

 You can see more examples of pinup fundraisers by visiting http://fwb40.us/14uCI5j or scan the QR code to view them on your smartphone or tablet.

CHAPTER SIXTEEN

Facebook Likes Fundraiser

A popular social networking tool for fundraising with businesses is the Facebook Like. Using Likes to raise money is a digital version of the action-triggered donation programs we discussed in Chapter 6. A like on the nonprofit's or businesses' Facebook page, or both, triggers a donation.

Facebook Like programs are win-win. The nonprofit raises money and both company and nonprofit potentially get a new, engaged fan on their Facebook page.

KRAFT AND IKEA USE FACEBOOK LIKES
TO HELP CAUSES

A good example of fundraising with Facebook Likes was the Kraft Fight Hunger Facebook page for Feeding America. "Liking" the page triggered one meal donation, and more donations were earned as fans answered football and food-related trivia questions through the *2 Minute Trivia Drill Game*.

The program generated a whopping 25 million meals for Feeding America food banks across the country.

An interesting variation on the traditional Facebook Like promotion was IKEA's *Bring Your Own Friends* (BYOF), an event with deals and giveaways that rewarded Facebook fans that invited their friends to join them at IKEA with a donation to Save the Children. See Figure 16.1.

There are two lessons from this program.

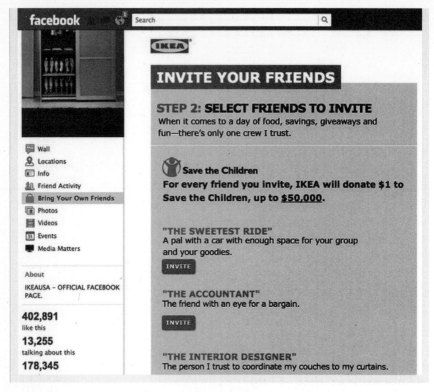

FIGURE 16.1

IKEA Donates a Dollar to Save the Children When You Invite a Friend to BYOF

First, it takes Facebook fundraising to a new level by using Facebook Likes to help drive what really matters to a retailer: in-store foot traffic. This is becoming a standard practice for businesses that are eager to turn Likes into customers.

Second, this promotion puts the nonprofit at just the right place—after the self-serving main offer of savings and giveaways, which is what really motivates shoppers. The donation to Save the Children is a secondary benefit, and the charity gets the money whether the invitee shows up or not.

HOW IT WORKS IN 1-2-3

1. Work with your business partner to decide whose Facebook page gets the Like (if not both), how much each one is worth, and how long the program will run.

2. The nonprofit and the business promote the fundraiser to their supporters and customers on Facebook and other online and offline channels (e.g., Twitter, e-mail, print newsletter, etc.).

3. At the end of the program, total the number of Likes received for the duration of the program and collect your donation from the company.

THINGS TO REMEMBER

- Don't make a fuss over how you got each Like. Just note the number of Likes you have at the beginning of the program, and subtract that number from the total you have at the end of the promotion. That's your total number of Likes and the number you'll use to collect your donation.

- Don't limit your promotion to Facebook. Promote the fundraiser in your printed and electronic e-mail newsletter, in e-mail signatures, on other social networks and at events.

- To have a successful Facebook Likes fundraiser, your nonprofit or your business partner—preferably both—needs to have a large, engaged following on Facebook to drive the program. If you have 50 fans on Facebook and your business partner has even fewer, your fundraiser will soon run out of gas.

- You'll need a plan after your fundraiser to keep new fans engaged and coming back to your page. Getting a Like is one thing. Keeping people interested and engaged requires a steady stream of powerful content that will cut through the clutter of Facebook's news feed. Looking for more information on how to successfully manage your Facebook page? One of the best books on the subject is *Facebook Marketing for Dummies* by John Haydon. You can also visit John online at http://johnhaydon.com.

Stop Focusing on Tools

We have all these tools—Facebook, computers, web sites, pinups, social networks, QR Codes, mobile technology—but we're not sure how they work or what they're for. Often times we expect them to do things they can't do.

A hammer doesn't make a home. Its job is to pound in a nail. It's a tool.

To be successful raising money with a business, you have to look beyond your toolbox to what you're actually trying to build.

It's only then that we can choose the right tool for the work ahead.

- Take a good look at your brand—that thing people feel when they come into contact with you. It's the #1 predictor of success.

- Analyze your assets. What is it about your nonprofit that makes it truly special, unique? What do you have that others envy? If you're not sure, ask them!

- Focus on things that work—the tangible, the measurable.

- Work on developing and telling your story.

- Before you try to construct or innovate anything, focus on the building blocks, the foundation.

- Stick with the basics. They work!

- Start with ideas. They'll drive your success better than any tool.

- Focus on a lasting value. Something that shines through and pervades everything you do.

(continued)

Tools cannot replace ideas, purpose, identity, results, and values. When we say a house has "character" we recognize the craft and art of the builder, not the tool that he or she used to make it.

It's time to choose. Do you want to be a builder or a hammer?

STEAL THESE IDEAS!

1. Instead of Likes, you may want to count *Shares*. Businesses are beginning to place a higher value on sharing over Likes. Scott Monty, social media director at Ford Motor Company, explained why to *Adweek*. "The Like, as far as I'm concerned, is the minimum commitment you can ask from a [Facebook] fan," he said. "Likes, comments, shares—it goes in that order of importance. Even the person who authors the first comment is Like an 'ugh,' another digital grunt. I am more interested in the value of a share." If your nonprofit has a good Facebook following, and, more importantly, good engagement, a company may *like* you more if you focus on *shares*.

2. Combine a Facebook Like fundraiser with an offline tactic. For example, in working with a business on a pinup (Chapter 15) or register fundraiser (Chapter 2), add a QR code that, when scanned, links to the company's or nonprofit's Facebook page. When the customer scans the code and Likes the page, the company makes an additional donation.

3. Facebook Like programs are easy to set up, which makes them easy to abuse by shortsighted companies and nonprofits. Shortly after a tornado devastated Moore, Oklahoma, killing 24 people, including school children, the Comfort Inn & Suites in Pottstown, Pennsylvania offered to donate a dollar—up to $1,000—for every Like it got on its Facebook page. This is self-serving nonsense. To tie Likes to donations so soon after a

tragedy, and to offer nothing if no Likes are received, is selfish, insensitive and very poor public relations. Complaints and pleas to end the promotion filled the hotel's Facebook page, which the hotel's social media manager deleted almost as quickly as people could write them. Disasters are bad enough. Don't make them worse by creating a public relations disaster for your nonprofit.

FOR MORE INFORMATION

 You can see more examples of Facebook Likes fundraisers by visiting http://fwb40.us/14ntld2 or scan the QR code to view them on your smartphone or tablet.

CHAPTER SEVENTEEN

Check-in to Give Fundraiser

If I were writing this chapter two years ago, I'd be gushing over about location-based networks and services like Loopt, Whrrl, Gowalla, SCVNGR, and others.

But that was two years ago. Today, many of these check-in services have closed and just a few key players remain.

However, that doesn't mean location-based services aren't a good fundraising option for businesses and nonprofits. Consider the following:

- Location-based networks have tens of millions of dedicated users that check in billions of times each year.

- The typical user is one of the most desirable demographics: young, college educated, and employed.

- It's marketing in people's pockets. You can share deals and specials with shoppers and they can refer businesses—and their nonprofit partners—to friends and family via Twitter and Facebook.

THREE WAYS TO CHECK-IN TO GIVE

Let's start with the three location-based services you should use for a check-in-to-give program.

Foursquare

Foursquare is the leading location-based social network. When people talk about "checking in" to a business, there's a good chance they're using the Foursquare mobile app.

Foursquare check-in to give fundraisers have been around for almost as long as Foursquare, which launched in 2009.

For example, during the holidays in 2012 luxury automaker Lexus launched *Check-In for Charity*. For each check-in from December 1 through January 2, Lexus donated $10 to Boys & Girls Clubs of America. Additionally, when Foursquare users checked in to a dealership, Lexus doubled the user's donation tally for the entire day.

Lexus raised $100,000 for Boys & Girls Clubs of America.

Facebook

Facebook added its own check-in to a business feature in 2010. The major difference between Foursquare and Facebook is the number of users. Although Foursquare has millions of worldwide users, Facebook has nearly a billion! Facebook has seen its share of check-in fundraisers as well.

For example, in 2011 outdoor retailer REI offered to donate $1 to a local nonprofit when Facebook users checked in to one of its 114 U.S. stores. A competitor, The North Face, took its promotion one step further by offering to donate $1 to the National Park Foundation for every check-in at its U.S. stores *and* at any one of America's nearly 400 national parks.

Check-in for Good

Check-in for Good is a cause-focused location-based service that rewards check-ins with donations to a cause. See Figure 17.1.

Like Foursquare and Facebook, it's a good option for businesses since the giving only happens when shoppers check-in to the business. An added bonus is that businesses can add a special or discount to its check-in page to further drive visits and donations.

HOW IT WORKS IN 1-2-3

1. Identify a business partner and choose a location-based platform (e.g. Foursquare, Facebook, etc.) for a check-in-to-give program.

FIGURE 17.1

When Customers Check-in, the Business Makes a Donation to a Nonprofit
Source: Courtesy of Checkinforgood.com.

2. Determine how much of the cash or product the company will donate with each check-in.

3. At the end of the program add up the number of check-ins and collect your donation.

THINGS TO REMEMBER

- You can keep track of check-ins in two ways. First, all three check-in services have back-end analytics for businesses that will track check-ins automatically. This is, by far, the easiest and fastest way to keep track of check-ins and donations.

- A second option is to ask users to push their check-in to Twitter with a hashtag or handle. For example, McDonald's restaurants in Philadelphia did this for a Foursquare fundraiser for the Ronald McDonald House Charities. McDonald's donated a dollar to the charity for every check-in that was sent to Twitter with the handle @McDPhilly. Users could also use the hashtag #McDPhilly. The benefit of this second option is the extra promotion you get on Twitter. It's also easy to track results on Twitter Search. The downside is you add an extra step, which may affect overall participation.

- Rob Katz, Founder of Check-in for Good, suggests you mass your forces. "Don't limit a check-in to give program to just one store," said Rob. "Involve a bunch of businesses at the same time. You want supporters to get into the habit of checking in for your cause."

- Rob also suggests that nonprofits take the lead in promoting the program with supporters. "When businesses see that you're committed to the program, they'll double their efforts," he said. "Promote the program everywhere—in your newsletter, e-mail, events, social media sites."

What You Need to Know Before You Check-in to a Location-Based Fundraiser

Check-in fundraisers with Foursquare, Facebook, or Check-in for Good aren't easy. The number of social media users that are active on these networks is, well, small. Experts surmise that fewer than 1 percent of all social media users are active on location-based services!

Still, check-in fundraisers are worthwhile and can succeed, so long as you can answer yes to these four questions.

1. **Are customers *inclined* to use location-based services?** Don't fool yourself into thinking that older shoppers will jump on Foursquare when you ask them to. They won't. Instead, answer this question: Are your business partner's customers smartphone-toting Millennials born after 1980? If they aren't, you can cross off a check-in fundraiser.

(continued)

2. **Are you an expert?** Most consumers aren't quite sure how location-based services work. Do you? If your nonprofit doesn't understand how they work or their value to a business, how do you plan to explain the opportunity to a business partner, who, in turn, has to explain it to a customer?

3. **Are you active on other social networks?** Organizations that are already blogging, tweeting, updating, and pinning are the best candidates for a check-in fundraiser. These organizations understand how social networks work and know how to form a strategy for your check-in fundraiser.

4. **Is your business partner prepared to offer customers a deal?** Shoppers will listen to an employee explain a service if they know something is in it for them. One of the great things about Check-in for Good is that you can easily add a deal or special to the check-in. This is a big incentive for customers.

I know what you're thinking. "Come on, Joe. Who's going to be able to answer yes to all four of these questions?" Not many, for sure. But the organizations that have done well with location-based services can answer yes to all four of these questions.

You have to do a gut check before you check-in to give.

STEAL THESE IDEAS!

1. Just because you're working with a business doesn't mean the check-in can't happen somewhere else. The North Face tied their donation to check-ins at national parks. EarthJustice had supporters check in to a billboard, which triggered a $10 gift. Supporters can check-in to events, TV shows, movies, books,

ads, or whatever you and your partner agree on. Marketers agree that checking into something besides a business may enhance the user's experience and connection with the brand. Checking in to a national park and seeing The North Face brand says more about a company and its values than a brick and mortar store does.

2. A good alternative to check-in to give is scan-to-give (see Chapter 20). Instead of checking in on Foursquare, Facebook, or Check-in for Good, the shopper scans a QR code to trigger a donation.

FOR MORE INFORMATION

 You can see more examples of check-in to give fund-raisers by visiting http://fwb40.us/17HFAya or scan the QR code to view them on your smartphone or tablet.

CHAPTER EIGHTEEN

Payroll Deduction

Payroll deduction is one of the oldest and more popular forms of business giving. Employees sign up for payroll deductions, choose a charity, and a percentage or portion of their pretax wages is regularly deducted and given to the charity.

The challenge with payroll deduction isn't getting the money from the company. It's getting on the company's list of eligible nonprofits.

As Adam Weinger of Double the Donation (www.doublethedonation.com), a website that helps nonprofits maximize corporative giving opportunities, explains: "Unfortunately the charitable options for employees may be limited to a preset list of eligible nonprofits that varies by company. *The challenge for each nonprofit is figuring out how to be included on those lists of eligible nonprofits.*"

Getting listed can be difficult but not impossible, and, according to Adam, well worth it. "Automatic payroll deductions are one of the few opportunities for your organization to secure an ongoing, predictable source of revenue."

WHAT EMPLOYEES WANT TO KNOW
BEFORE THEY GIVE

The beauty and challenge of payroll deduction is that employees have many nonprofits to choose from. They can afford to be picky, and the charity they support this year can be easily replaced the following year.

Here are some of the questions employees will have before they support you—or support you again.

Is your organization making a difference?

As donors, employees want to know that your organization is making a difference in the issue they care about. If your nonprofit helps the elderly, be clear on how many people you aid, where they live in the community, and how you help them. Never miss an opportunity to show how your organization is having an impact. If employees never hear from you, there's a good chance you'll never hear from them—or their money.

How much of my money will support your mission?

Payroll deduction programs are very cost efficient. It's one of the reasons why so many companies and employees use them. They feel good knowing that most of the money goes to the nonprofit, and not to covering expenses. They want the same feeling when the money gets to your organization. If more than 20 cents of every dollar donated is going to expenses and overhead, you should be clear with employees on why it costs more to run your organization.

Will you make it easy for me to give?

Donating to a cause through payroll deduction is a snap for employees, but they may need your help to keep it easy. If an employee contributes $250 or more from a single paycheck, then they must prove to the IRS that they didn't receive anything in return for it. Nonprofits need to be diligent about monitoring who these donors are and supplying them with the documentation they need to confirm they didn't receive any goods or services in return for their gift.

Take this chance to inform donors you are making tax time easier for them! They'll appreciate the support and may continue theirs.

Is your charity a "good" one?

Employees have so many nonprofits to choose from there's a good chance they'll do their own research. Does your website give them the information they need? Is it easy to find? How well is your charity rated on review sites such as Charity Navigator? Take off your rose-colored glasses and see how employees will view your organization among the hundreds of others they can support instead.

Are there other ways I can help you?

Employees that support your nonprofit through payroll deduction may be willing to support it in other ways. Make sure employees know about other giving options within their company, such as matching gifts (Chapter 29) and dollars for doers (Chapter 36). Also, give them a way to participate in your events, either as a volunteer or attendee.

HOW IT WORKS IN 1-2-3

1. Your nonprofit gets listed as a selection in the company's charity payroll deduction program.

2. Employees choose a charity, a donation level and a frequency for their gift (usually weekly, but it could be monthly or even one time).

3. After a year, the employee reviews his or her choice and donation and adjusts as desired.

THINGS TO REMEMBER

- Larger companies and organizations often have "Giving Fairs" where employees can meet nonprofits and learn about their missions. This is a great opportunity to be more than a name in a giving directory.

- Take advantage of any opportunity your organization might have to speak to employees. Leave an impression by asking someone who has benefited from your mission to speak with you. Potential donors don't want or need to hear from nonprofit administrators. They want to hear from the people you help and need your organization.

- All payroll deduction programs have an application process. Be sure to complete your application well before the deadline, as many other nonprofits will be vying for approval. The number one reason an application is denied? It's incomplete.

Don't Shoot the Messenger

Some people extol the virtues of "hidden charity." These saints don't give to get their name on a building, or to receive a special gift or a shopping bag full of coupons. They give because the rewards transcend the material and common-place. They give because it's right and good and noble.

The fundraisers I write about in this book are the opposite of "hidden charity" because they are promotional for the business. Some people would call them selfish, opportunistic, or showy.

Although there are many good examples of fundraisers with businesses, the bad ones seem to get all the attention. The latter is generally a result of bad or misguided values, not poor practices. The 2010 fundraiser between Komen for the Cure and Kentucky Fried Chicken wasn't a failure of practices—in this case pink buckets from which 50 cents was donated to Komen—but a byproduct of bad values and even poorer choices.

Monies raised from business fundraisers can be real gifts when good intentions drive practices.

Instead, we shoot the messenger.

Regardless of the type of fundraiser, people give for both the right and wrong reasons. Like the collection plates I saw passed at church when I was a kid, businesses are there to enable and to collect donations, not to measure, evaluate, or judge. We should let these businesses do their job and devote our time to teaching people the real meaning of charity.

You may know of a company and cause partnership that flowed from caring to commerce. I do.

For seven years I worked with a man who ran a chain of discount retailers based in New England. He supported my nonprofit in many ways— some private, some public. Frankly, it really didn't matter which. Regardless of how he chose to

(continued)

support us, his generosity didn't flow from his "hidden" side on one day and public on the next. It came from *his charity*.

Charity can only be found in the giver, and that's where our work in society lies. We have to convince people of the core reason to give, which is to be a part of something bigger than themselves and to serve the public good.

Charity stems from *why* people want to give, not the how and what they give. Fundraisers with businesses are just another chance for people to give and to change the world.

STEAL THESE IDEAS!

1. When you say payroll deduction, everyone thinks of the United Way. But you have other options. Join one or all the organizations that set up giving campaigns at corporations. Here is a list of possibilities:
   - America's Charities
   - Earth Share
   - Community Shares USA
   - Community Health Charities
   - Combined Federal Campaign

2. As with most fundraising strategies, incentives work with payroll deduction. When the St. Louis United Way offered incentives to employee campaign coordinators who exceeded their company's goals by a certain threshold from the previous year, the United Way saw an average 10 percent increase in their overall giving from 2011. There was also a 15 percent increase in employee participation from 2012.

3. If a company doesn't have a payroll deduction program, encourage employees to set up their own weekly donation program using Razoo, Network for Good, First Giving, or

another online giving platform. Just remember that your donation will be with after-tax dollars, instead of pre-tax.

4. If your business partner doesn't have a payroll deduction program, encourage them to set one up. Working with their payroll provider, companies can set up a simple program to support their favorite charities, including yours.

5. Coordinators of payroll deduction programs are always in need of speakers for kick-off events. Make sure they know that you're available to speak, even if it's last minute. "We get a lot fewer calls than you think from nonprofits asking if they can speak at an event," said Duke Hutchinson, a campaign manager for the Charitable Federal Campaign (CFC) in Boston. "Often we're scrambling at the last minute to find a suitable speaker for a kickoff."

6. On the public side of charitable payroll deduction, you have the CFC for federal employees. But state and city employees have their own payroll deduction programs you need to apply for separately. For example, in my home state of Massachusetts there is the Charitable Federal Campaign for federal workers, the Commonwealth of Massachusetts Employee Charitable Campaign (COMECC) for state employees, and the City of Boston Employee Charitable Campaign (COBECC) for city workers. Three different programs with three different pools of money!

FOR MORE INFORMATION

 You can see more examples of payroll deduction programs by visiting http://fwb40.us/164Yal5 or scan the QR code to view them on your smartphone or tablet.

CHAPTER NINETEEN

Sports Team Fundraiser

We all know that professional sports teams are businesses. But we really don't treat them like one, do we? We think of them more as celebrities that come to our events and sign things for auctions.

But sports teams can offer a lot more than star appeal, or a signed baseball. I learned this firsthand in a partnership with the Bruins, Boston's National Hockey League team, a few years back.

In this chapter, we'll look at how your local sports teams can deliver a lot more than a famous face, and how you don't need to be a marquee nonprofit to score with them.

HOW I LEARNED TO GIVE A PUCK ABOUT
SPORTS TEAM FUNDRAISING

I was really looking forward to my meeting with the Boston Bruins. Waiting for the director of community relations in the TD Bank Garden where the team plays, I wasn't admiring the Bruins' championship banners hanging from the rafters. I was looking at all the sponsors surrounding the rink.

"Forget about solid ice. More like solid gold," I thought greedily. "If I can get the Bruins to introduce me to just a few of these sponsors, it will be like my nonprofit won a championship!"

I must have been glowing when I sat down with the community relations director because he immediately dimmed my lights.

"We're happy to work with your organization, but our current sponsors and corporate partners are off the table," he said.

My heart sank. "Okay," I said. "What did you have in mind?" My mind turned to what I would do with that signed hockey stick I'd probably get.

Thankfully, he had bigger plans than that. He explained that although he couldn't share his business partners with me, he could share other things.

- The Bruins had a rabid fan following, and maybe finding that Bruins fan in the corporate world would be the key to winning a new business partner. He just needed to give us the right things to woo them.

- The Bruins often played to a full house at The Garden and the Jumbotron and check presentations on the ice would put my organization and our business partners in front of tens of thousands of people. See Figure 19.1. The Bruins were also happy to host a group of supporters in one of their luxury boxes. This was a nice perk for a C-level executive who was also a hockey fan.

FIGURE 19.1

Who doesn't want to be in a picture with a big check? That's me, second from left with the Bruins and my corporate partners

- The Bruins were willing to commit to a limited number of player appearances at businesses that met ambitious fund-raising goals for our organization.

The Bruins didn't give me money or connections, but they did give me *assets*—things I could use with business prospects to raise money.

Shortly after meeting with the Bruins, I recruited two new company partners to work with my organization. They were excited about working with the hometown team. In a town known for baseball, I had found two hockey fans!

Together, we raised $42,000 the first year, and we matched that number the second year.

HOW IT WORKS IN 1-2-3

1. Identify a sports team to work with and do an asset analysis of the things you could use for a partnership. Rank these from probable (e.g., free tickets to game) to difficult or improbable (e.g., player appearances, text-to-give fundraiser on the Jumbotron).

2. Approach the sports team about working with them and leveraging their assets. Stress how turnkey the program is (i.e., You'll do all the work!) and how the fundraiser will deliver a good promotional return for a minimum investment of resources.

3. Take the assets you collected from the sports team and market them to potential corporate partners. Target senior executives that support the sports team! See *Steal These Ideas!* in this chapter for more information on how to identify business owners who are also sports fans.

THINGS TO REMEMBER

- Sports teams don't have a lot of time for handholding, especially during their respective season of play. That's why you need to be the creator and driver of the program. If you're not, no one will be.

- It's best to approach sports teams in the off-season when they are planning for the upcoming season.

- A lot of sports teams have established charitable programs for nonprofits. They have guidelines for getting things like signed balls, bats, and helmets. Take advantage of these programs knowing that you'll be dealing with a separate part of the front office. In short, accepting these items won't keep you from accessing other assets from the team. This chapter poses a whole different opportunity for your nonprofit.

Four Ways to Cross the Fundraising Finish Line Faster

Nonprofits share a common goal with their for-profit counter-parts: they want to close more deals as quickly as possible. But it's not easy these days. Businesses are looking for a more consultative approach from nonprofit partners. And, truthfully, the economy is giving everyone a good excuse not to act quickly.

But you can buck inertia if you approach the process more like a marathon. That means shortening your stride to meet the long and challenging road ahead.

Here are four ways to close more deals by being prepared, novel, persistent, and practical.

1. Stay Prospect-Centric

Always be prepared to adjust your messaging to meet a prospect's needs, interests, and goals. You may have just spoken to three prospects that were happy to focus on the benefits of working with you, but can you make the shift when the next prospect wants to talk about your nonprofit's mission? You have to adjust your pitch accordingly to keep their attention and realize their potential as a prospect.

(continued)

2. Stand Out from Your Competition

Sadly, most business people have pretty low expectations of nonprofit types. They expect you to ask for money, and to bring little else to the table except your empty, cupped hands. Act differently. Don't ask for something; start by offering something (e.g., the opportunity to reach a key demographic such as moms). Enlighten them on how supporting a cause can deliver a competitive edge and boost employee morale, among other things. Show them you know something about their industry, challenges and competitors.

You know what the average fundraiser does (that person may even be you!), step out from what's expected and you'll get some unexpected attention from businesses.

3. Don't Give Them an Excuse to Say No

These are pet peeves of mine: mailing prospects reams of information, not calling people back when you said you would, presenting programs that lack research and creativity. These are all excuses (no, good reasons!) for a prospect to say "no". You never want to get a flat-out "no" from a prospect. Psychologically, it's a big threshold for a decision maker to cross and when they do say "no", well, they generally mean it. So why would you want to do something dumb that will hasten a negative, perhaps fatal response? Think about it.

4. Persuasion Is Incremental

These things take time. It's not going to happen with one call, or with one e-mail, or with one meeting. You need to plan for success and how each step will bring you closer to it. So if the objective of that first call isn't to seal the deal, what is it? It's a question you should know the answer to before you ever pick up the phone.

It's early in the race. Pace yourself.

STEAL THESE IDEAS!

1. It's no coincidence that I had luck with Boston's professional hockey team. Boston is a town full of great sports teams. The top three are the Boston Red Sox, The New England Patriots and the Boston Celtics. Boston loves its hockey, but hockey is not the city's first, second, or even third love. It's almost impossible for a nonprofit to get a meeting with the Red Sox. The Bruins are more receptive because they need the marketing more than the Sox do. What sports teams in your area needs help? Professional hockey is slowly spreading across the southern United States. Perhaps you, too, would have more luck with your hockey team than, say, with your champion professional football team. It depends on your community. Also, what about sports that are growing in popularity like soccer, lacrosse, women's football, and ultimate Frisbee? These sports need good partners as much as your nonprofit does.

2. You're probably wondering how you can identify business owners that are sports fans. You can gather this information from a variety of places, but what's important is what you do with the information once you have it. That's why every nonprofit office should have donor management software. As you read through your local business pages and journals and network at your local Chamber of Commerce and other events, you'll record this information in your database. You'll be surprised how much you can learn talking to people at events and reading about them online or in the newspaper. Focus as much on the personal information as the professional. Passions, like sports, will tell you as much about a prospect as where they worked or went to school. When I walked into the Boston Garden to talk to the Bruins, I wasn't sure what I'd get from them. But I knew that whatever it was, I'd have a business in my database to call when I got back to the office.

3. If your nonprofit needs coats, food, or anything else, sporting events are a great place for a collection drive. A local food bank

teamed up with a supermarket and a minor league baseball team for a mac and cheese challenge. Fans brought boxes of mac and cheese, which made great noisemakers during the game!

FOR MORE INFORMATION

 You can see more examples of sports team fund-raisers by visiting http://fwb40.us/1fEXEM1 or scan the QR code to view them on your smartphone or tablet.

CHAPTER TWENTY

Scan-to-Give Fundraiser

You've probably seen more than your share of QR codes. They seem to be popping up everywhere—magazines, direct mail, billboards, resumes, and even as tattoos on people's bodies.

I clearly remember the first time I saw a QR code. Puzzled, I thought it looked like an aerial view of a cornfield maze created by farmers—or perhaps aliens!

Fortunately, QR codes are not the work of mischievous farmers or aliens. But their potential for fundraising with businesses may be out of this world!

SIX WAYS TO USE QR CODES TO RAISE MONEY

Here are six ways nonprofits can use QR codes to raise money with businesses.

1. **QR code links to PayPal.** After scanning the QR code, the user enters her PayPal username and password to process the donation.

    Advantage: The user can quickly make a donation without manually entering her credit card information.

    Disadvantage: The user has to have a PayPal account.

    Real-Life Example: Baked-goods chain Cinnabon posted QR codes at its registers and encouraged customers to scan and give to antihunger organization Share Our Strength via PayPal. The campaign raised $3,800.

2. **QR code links to a merchant account.** After scanning the QR code, the user enters his credit-card information.

Advantage: Anyone with a credit card can make a donation.

Disadvantage: You have to type in your credit card number every time you make a mobile donation (A huge pain!).

Real-Life Example: Big Brothers Big Sisters of Kansas City used a QR code that linked to a mobile site where users could enter their credit card information and make a donation.

3. **QR code links to text-to-give.** After scanning the QR code, the user charges the donation to her cell phone account.

   Advantage: A quick and easy solution! Plus, most users are comfortable with text so there's no learning curve.

   Disadvantage: Text-to-give plans vary, but in general, it will be your most expensive option.

   Real-Life Example: Beer maker *50 Back* used a QR code to link to a landing page where users could buy a solider a beer for $1.99. See Figure 20.1. Text2Pay handled donations. The user's cellphone account was charged $1.99, but Text2Pay took $.99 of every purchase as a processing fee. In less than a year, 50 Back gave away 7,400 beers to thirsty soldiers.

4. **QR code triggers a cash or in-kind donation.** After scanning the QR code, the business will donate cash or product to a nonprofit.

FIGURE **20.1**

Text-to-Give with This QR Code and Donate a Beer to a Soldier!
Source: Courtesy of 50 Back.

Advantage: Like the clicks on a hyperlink, it's easy to track the number of times a QR code is scanned.

Disadvantage: The user isn't given the opportunity to support the campaign beyond scanning the QR code. The company, not the consumer, makes the donation. Consumers may feel like this simple action isn't making a real difference.

Real-Life Example: When you scan the QR code on the back of a Heinz Ketchup bottle and thank a veteran for their service, Heinz will donate $1 to the Wounded Warriors Project.

5. **QR code links to a contest site that rewards nonprofits that get the most votes.** After scanning the QR code, the user votes for the nonprofit project she wants the company to support.

Advantage: The consumer plays an active and important role in choosing a nonprofit that deserves support.

Disadvantage: The investment needed to create a mobile voting site may be beyond the means of most small nonprofits.

Real-Life Example: Sonic *Limeades for Learning* to benefit Donorschoose.org featured a QR code on cups that led users to a mobile site where they could vote for their favorite school project across the country. Weekly, Sonic donated $100,000 to the most-voted projects.

6. **QR code on a mobile payment app allows you to donate to causes within the app.** Mobile payment app LevelUp lets users turn savings into donations for causes.

Advantage: An easy way to support a cause.

Disadvantage: You can only earn savings points from businesses that accept the LevelUp app.

Real-Life Example: LevelUp lets you choose the percentage of savings and the charity that will receive the donation.

HOW IT WORKS IN 1-2-3

1. Working with your business partner, pick the type of scan-to-give program you want to execute.

2. Create a QR code, a mobile landing page, if needed, and promote the fundraiser.

3. Track the number of scans, votes, or redemptions and collect your donation.

THINGS TO REMEMBER

- Test, test, test. Once you've created a QR code for a fundraiser, test it at the exact location it will be used to make sure it works. Poor lighting or a lousy cell signal can doom your QR code and fundraiser before it ever gets started.

- Test your QR code with different smartphones to make sure it works with different models and versions.

- Think about who scans QR codes. It's not your grandfather—unless he happens to be hip and cool. Thirty percent of 18- to 34-year-olds have used QR codes in the past year. Are QR code users your business partner's customers?

- Train the company's employees on what QR codes are and how to use them. If a customer is curious about QR codes but doesn't know how to scan one, businesses should be prepared to show them how to download a QR code reader and scan the code.

Raising Money with Coupons, QR Codes

Despite marketers' hopes that consumers would scan QR codes to learn more about products and services, people prefer to scan them to—surprise, surprise—get deals and save money. The lesson here is that, when it comes to sharing coupons with shoppers, QR codes are a good option.

The extra incentive to scan the QR code and follow through on using the coupon is the cause component. Consumers—particularly moms and millennials—are more likely to buy something when it's connected to a cause.

(continued)

Mixing QR codes, coupons, and fundraising makes a lot of sense. Here's how to do it.

Step 1: Recruit a business to support the program

Since the donation is tied to the consumer redeeming the coupon, you'll need to decide on a donation per redemption and a cap for the program. For instance, for every coupon redeemed, the business owner will donate 25 cents up to $2,500. Businesses are happy to help, but no one wants to trigger a Groupon-like nightmare that would punish the business with too many redemptions.

Step 2: Create a QR code

There are plenty of free QR Code generators on the web, but be sure to pick a quality generator that allows you to create a QR Code, to change what it links to without changing the code itself and to track the number of scans. I've been happy with a paid service, uQR.me (http://uqr.me), for creating and tracking my QR Codes, but there are plenty of other options if you search for them.

Step 3: Create a mobile page with Google Sites

Your QR code will link to a mobile-ready site that will explain the offer. I'm sure there are other options, but I checked out Google Sites (http://sites.google.com) and, although it is basic, it's a good first stop for mobile site design. It's also free. When creating the mobile site you'll need to decide whether a QR code or other type of barcode should be included on the mobile landing page. This is critical because you'll need to determine how redemptions will be tracked. Will the cashier scan a QR code or barcode to record the redemption (and thus your donation), or will they keep track of it in some other way? One option is to ask the business owner to award the donation whenever the QR code is scanned (which is different from linking the donation to when the coupon is used at the register).

(continued)

(*continued*)

Step 4: Promote the offer

The final step is to promote the heck out of your QR code coupon. Your business partner can help. Nonprofits can promote and distribute the coupon to their supporters, but, a word of caution: some states aren't too keen on letting nonprofits promote their for-profit partnerships. You should speak to your state's attorney general's office, and then weigh the risks/rewards before moving forward.

I like to know the law before I decide to break it. So should you.

STEAL THESE IDEAS!

1. You can include a scan-to-give in a larger fundraising program. For example, in 2011 Chili's Grill & Bar added QR codes to coloring sheets and table tents created for the *Create-a-Pepper to Fight Childhood Cancer* program to benefit St. Jude Children's Research Hospital. But to enhance the impact of the program, Chili's also sold *Create-A-Pepper* merchandise (aka signature cause product, see Chapter 33) and held a donate profits day (see Chapter 27). The QR codes served as an extra resource for how people could get involved and donate to St. Jude.

2. Add a QR code to your pinup so people can learn more about your nonprofit when they donate. More customers are asking at the register: "What am I giving to? How much of my donation will the charity receive?" A QR code informs and educates and opens the door to more engagement with your organization.

3. Did you know that most QR codes are scanned at work and at home? Use a QR code on thank-you letters and in newsletters to deliver a personal thank you to an individual or company

donor. Record a special thank-you from a client thanking donors. If you work for an animal shelter, record a few minutes of puppies playing. To thank a special donor, mention them *by name* in the video.

FOR MORE INFORMATION

 You can see more examples of scan-to-give fundraisers by visiting http://fwb40.us/1dZfmOH or scan the QR code to view them on your smartphone or tablet.

CHAPTER TWENTY-ONE

Shop-Walk Fundraiser

A shop-walk is a shopping fundraiser that happens at multiple businesses in the same area on the same day. For example, in the aftermath of the Boston Marathon bombing, salons and shops in Boston's Back Bay hosted a shop-walk to help stylist Celeste Corcoran who, along with her daughter, Sydney, was severely injured in the blast.

For the *Boston Strong Celeste-a-thon* on May 13, 2013, each participating shop offered a percentage or portion of sales from the day's sales or from a specific product or service. For example, a dry cleaner offered to donate 10 percent of the day's receipts. The salon at which Celeste worked donated 100 percent on everything from haircuts to manicures. Two dozen businesses participated and raised more than $120,000 for Celeste.

Shop-walks have a festive, supportive vibe as shoppers walk from store to store taking advantage of deals and supporting a good cause. They truly put the *fun* in fundraising!

RAISING MONEY FROM SMALL BUSINESSES WITH SHOPPING DAYS

Are you a local nonprofit that has a downtown business district full of mom and pop stores? Shopping days may be the fundraiser for you. There are three components to a shopping day program.

- Pinups (Chapter 15)
- Percentage-of-sales (Chapter 1)
- Shop-walk

Here's how they all work together.

Working with your small business partners, pick a day or weekend to have a shopping-day event. Prior to the event, downtown businesses agree to sell pinups or donate a percentage or portion of sales from a product or service (or do both). The goal is to help raise money for your organization and to promote the shopping day.

To make this program work, you'll need to secure one more thing from your business partners: a discount for shoppers that participate in the shopping-day fundraiser.

While your business partners are promoting your fundraiser, your nonprofit will be busy recruiting walkers. In the shop-walk I organized, we asked walkers to raise a minimum of $250. In exchange, walkers received a pink canvas bag with the shop-walk logo on it. See Figure 21.1. The bag was all they needed to receive discounts at participating stores.

Everyone wins with a shopping day. The nonprofit raises money. The business owner gets foot traffic and hopefully new customers. Walkers have a great time raising money for your organization and saving money on their purchases.

A good example of a shopping-day fundraiser in action is *Shop Local for a Cause* from the National Association of Local Advertisers (NALA) that benefits The Greatest Generation Foundation, a nonprofit dedicated to promoting recognition and respect for U.S. and Allied war veterans of past and current conflicts.

NALA gives small businesses all the tools they needed to host a shopping day event. Percentage-of-sales programs (Chapter 1) were a popular option with business partners.

FIGURE 21.1

This Logo on our Shop-Walk Bags Triggered Store Discounts for Shoppers

No large businesses or chains in your area? No problem. Shopping days are perfect for a downtown business district.

HOW IT WORKS IN 1-2-3

1. The business partner agrees to host a fundraising event from which your nonprofit will receive a portion or percentage of the total sales from purchases that day.
2. The nonprofit and the business promote the fundraiser to supporters and customers.
3. The day of the event, the business tracks purchases and donates a percentage of the total sales, or a portion of the sales from specific customers (e.g., shoppers who identify themselves as supporters of your nonprofit), to your nonprofit.

THINGS TO REMEMBER

- The key to shop-walk success is massing your forces. Instead of working with one small business on a solo fundraiser, you consolidate businesses for one large fundraiser. Direct your firepower on one objective.
- Be flexible on what businesses can offer the day of the shop-walk. Every business is different and what a bank does will be different from what a clothing store can do. Think of how you can maximize every opportunity. In the shop-walk that I ran, a restaurant offered to donate food so we added a luncheon to our event to thank our top donors.

Has Your Fundraising Lost Its Magic? Here's How to Make It Reappear

One of my favorite movies is *The Prestige* (2006). Set in nineteenth-century London, the movie depicts the rivalry of two talented magicians, played by Hugh Jackman and
(continued)

(*continued*)

Christian Bale. It's a great movie, and has an ending I promise you'll love.

The movie opens and ends with the words of "Cutter," a character played by veteran actor Michael Caine.

Cutter describes the three parts or acts of every great magic trick. But his description isn't limited to illusionists who make things disappear and reappear. It's true for every field that takes something ordinary, does something extraordinary, but then has to prove that it wasn't a fluke, a sleight of hand, and can make it reappear again.

That's true magic:

> Every great magic trick consists of three parts or acts.
>
> The first part is called "The Pledge." The magician shows you something ordinary: a deck of cards, a bird or a man. He shows you this object. Perhaps he asks you to inspect it to see if it is indeed real, unaltered, normal. But of course . . . it probably isn't.
>
> The second act is called "The Turn." The magician takes the ordinary something and makes it do something extraordinary. Now you're looking for the secret . . . but you won't find it, because of course you're not really looking. You don't really want to know. You want to be fooled. But you wouldn't clap yet. Because making something disappear isn't enough; you have to bring it back.
>
> That's why every magic trick has a third act, the hardest part, the part we call "The Prestige."

"The Prestige" of business fundraising happens when we take an ordinary nonprofit and for-profit partnership and turn it into something special. This means doing it more than once. You have to bring it back again and again.

Here are four tips to ensure that your first business fundraiser isn't your last.

1. Educate Your Partner

Even after a successful fundraiser, don't just assume your partner is sold on helping you. Continue to educate them on the benefits of working with you and how it helps *their* business.

(*continued*)

2. Establish Points of Value

What criteria will the two of you use to determine the success of the fundraiser? Will it be dollars raised, or will customer and employee feedback be the metric? What about sales? Is the business expecting the program to drive revenue? Don't assume your metric for success is the same as your business partner's. Clarify expectations at the start and make sure they're fulfilled. Refine and repeat.

3. Work Their Circle

Every business has a circle of influence, connections with other businesses that they can leverage to support a nonprofit. Can you tap these prospects to grow your fundraiser? You won't know until you ask. Don't let reticence undermine a potential growth strategy.

4. It's About Philanthro-tunity

Every business partner has something special, something valuable to offer. And it's not always about money. I used to work with a large pizza chain that offered to supply my business partners with pizzas as incentives and rewards for employees and stores that exceeded their fundraising goals.

Most nonprofits feel lucky if they execute one successful fundraiser with a business. But the magic happens when you can bring it back again and again and again. That's the hardest part of a fundraising program.

That's why I call it "The Prestige."

STEAL THESE IDEAS!

1. Shop-walks generally involve businesses in one area. But don't exclude other businesses that may want to participate. For example, for Boston's Celeste-a-thon, businesses throughout eastern Massachusetts were eager to participate and ran their own promotion. It made for a bigger event, got people

involved that couldn't make it downtown and raised more money for Celeste.

2. Pinups (Chapter 15) are a great way to promote your events and raise money. In the weeks before your shop-walk, ask participating stores to sell pinups at the register. On the pinup, include a takeaway or tear-off that promotes the date of the shop-walk. You can even include an extra incentive, such as a free service or discount when shoppers redeem a coupon found only on the pinup.

3. Organize a *cause mob* as part of your shop-walk. You may have already heard of a *cash mob*, which involves a group of consumers supporting a local business. But as UK corporate fundraising consultant John Thompson pointed out in *UK Fundraising* (www.fundraising.co.uk), a *cash mob* could be turned into a *cause mob* with people spending money at a business that has agreed to donate a portion of sales to a good cause. A cause mob could also be part of a shopping fundraiser (Chapter 5).

FOR MORE INFORMATION

 You can see more examples of shop-walk fundraisers by visiting http://fwb40.us/15DXdNe or scan the QR code to view them on your smartphone or tablet.

CHAPTER TWENTY-TWO

Collection Drive

Collection drives have been around for as long as people have had stuff to give away to those less fortunate. Over the past century, businesses have taken the lead in collecting everything from scrap metal to winter coats to food.

In addition to having employees that can support the drives, businesses often offer convenient drop-off locations for consumers that are eager to combine giving with another activity, such as replacing what they just gave away with a purchase.

The international charity Oxfam has even coined a name for the intersection of donating used clothing where you can buy new ones. They call it *Shwopping*.

FIVE EXAMPLES OF COLLECTION DRIVES

Regardless of what you call them, collection drives in businesses are an easy way to engage employees and consumers in collecting much-needed items for nonprofits.

One Warm Coat and Burlington Coat Factory

Since 2007, Burlington Coat Factory, ABC-TV's *Good Morning America* and One Warm Coat have teamed up for *The Warm Coats and Warm Hearts Coat Drive*. The retail chain with 500 locations and the national nonprofit that provides coats to the needy, have collected and distributed over a million gently worn coats through the program.

Burlington Coat Factory thanks consumers for their donations with a coupon for 10 percent off their next purchase. See Figure 22.1.

FIGURE 22.1

Burlington Coat Factory and *Good Morning America* Support One Warm Coat
Source: Courtesy of One Warm Coat.

Good Morning America promotes the program via an on-air coat drive starting in November.

Seattle Seahawks and Toys for Tots Foundation

At a December game versus the Arizona Cardinals, fans got to donate unwrapped toys or cash at all gates to Toys for Tots' annual holiday drive.

Joining the Seahawks and Toys for Tots in the drive was Bekins Moving and Storage Co., which supplied staff and trucks to transport the toys.

Balfour Beatty Construction and Valentines for Veterans

For three years, the San Diego office of Balfour Beatty Construction has worked with area schools to create, collect, and distribute Valentine's Day cards to veterans at various military hospitals.

School children made the heartfelt notes—over 2,000 personalized cards and bookmarks—and helped deliver the items.

Many patients also received gift bags filled with playing cards, snacks, pencils, and magazines, the donation of which Balfour coordinated.

Red Robin Salutes U.S. Troops Stationed Abroad

For 10 days in February, Red Robin restaurants in eastern Pennsylvania collected basic supplies and food to ship to U.S. soldiers stationed overseas. Customers donated all sorts of items ranging from food to books to batteries.

Dress Barn and Dress for Success

For over a decade, 825 Dress Barn stores across the country have teamed up with Dress for Success to gather 60,000 articles of clothing as part of its S.O.S.—Send One Suit—Weekend donation drive.

Dress for Success distributes the new and used suits collected nationwide to women trying to return to the workforce.

HOW IT WORKS IN 1-2-3

1. Working with your business partner, identify an item(s) to collect and a start and end date of the drive.
2. Promote the collection drive to the businesses' employees and customers and to your supporters. Remember, incentivizing consumers with coupons and discounts will increase donations.
3. Pick up your donated items.

THINGS TO REMEMBER

- Your nonprofit will need to work closely with the business to coordinate pickup. Many companies hesitate on collection drives because they'll be overwhelmed with "stuff." Assure the business you can handle the demand and will provide prompt pickup.

- Like other fundraisers, collection drives need a goal. Keep track of how many coats, shoes, food products, and so on, you collect. For example, Dress for Success aims to collect 15,000 pieces of professional clothing per day. Having a goal motivates employees and donors.

- Promote the drive outside the business. In-store promotion helps, but use newsletters, Facebook, and advertising circulars, if applicable, to spread the word. If customers only hear about the opportunity when they're in the store, "next time" may never come.

When It Comes to Building Relationships, Talk Is Cheap

A series of three posts on the *Harvard Business Review* blog in 2010 by members of the Corporate Executive Board explored some of the myths surrounding consumer-buying decisions.

The authors concluded that consumers, more than ever, want a simple buying process that gets them the things they want and need without hype or excessive interactions.

Nonprofits can learn a thing or two from these findings, especially about stakeholder preferences for interactions.

But, first, a reality check.

Myth 1: Everyone Loves You

Despite our best attempts to believe otherwise, most people don't want a relationship with your nonprofit.

(continued)

The gift comes in response to a request from a friend or colleague, or for a write-off. These people don't really care about your organization. They just gave you some money.

Of course, there are others who really do care about your organization. The key is to know the difference between the two and to interact with them accordingly. Just don't think that more is better, because it's not.

Myth 2: Talking Builds the Relationship

It doesn't. Instead of just talking with stakeholders, focus on having a strategic conversation with them about your shared values. For example, I've always admired the anti-hunger organization Share Our Strength. I was a "free lunch" kid myself, and I support Share Our Strength's goal to feed America's kids. These shared values cement the relationship. According to the Corporate Executive Board, of the consumers who said they had a brand relationship, 64 percent cited shared values as the primary reason.

The message for nonprofits is clear: talk is cheap. Shared values and messaging is what gets donors' attention and keeps them coming back.

Myth 3: More Interactions Are Better

Over communicating with supporters doesn't work either. You're just drowning the donor in a sea of talk. If I follow a new person on Twitter and they clog up my stream with too many tweets, I'll ignore or unfollow him—even if some of his tweets are interesting and helpful. We have to choose our interactions carefully and value our connection with the donor.

As a marketer it's almost heresy to say it, but we have to remove frequency as a factor in donor communications. The Corporate Executive Board suggests asking if the communication is "going to reduce the cognitive overload consumers feel as they shop my category? If the answer is 'no' or 'not sure,' go back to the drawing board."

STEAL THESE IDEAS!

1. As with all the fundraisers in this book, consider offering incentives. For example, in its partnership with One Warm Coat, Burlington Coat Factory gives customers that donate coats 10 percent off their entire purchase.

2. To promote your collection drive, combine it with a pinup program (Chapter 15) that includes a tear-off for customers that mention the drive and the incentive for donating.

3. If you're working with a retailer, turn your collection drive into an event that includes a fashion or trunk show. If you're working with a restaurant, turn it into a reception or party for donors. Regardless of the business you're working with, make it fun!

4. Even if your nonprofit doesn't need the items collected from a drive, how would you like to get the money from the sale of them? Women's clothing retailer Eileen Fisher collects gently used Eileen Fisher clothes and sells them in its stores. The monies raised go to charity—and good, fashionable clothes are saved from landfills! You could suggest a similar program to a business.

5. You can collect other things for cash. With an electronics recycling fundraiser you collect cell phones, computers, game consoles, digital cameras, MP3 players, tablets, and so forth and exchange them for cold, hard cash! Use Google to find recyclers in your area. Or start with one of the largest fund-raising through recycling providers, FundingFactory.com.

FOR MORE INFORMATION

 You can see more examples of collection drives by visiting http://fwb40.us/1arbF2I or scan the QR code to view them on your smartphone or tablet.

CHAPTER TWENTY-THREE

Trade Show Fundraiser

According to the Center for Exhibition Research (CEIR), there are over 13,000 events in the United States each year with at least 3,000 net square feet of exhibit space per event. There are hundreds of thousands more meetings, conferences and congresses.

Trade shows are big business, so it's no surprise that savvy companies and causes are working together to raise money and make a difference.

FIVE EXAMPLES OF TRADE SHOW FUNDRAISERS

Trade show exhibitors engage booth visitors with everything from canned sales pitches to t-shirts to candy. But demonstrating their commitment to a cause may be the takeaway that conference goers keep.

Gerber Gear and Boy Scouts of America

At the Shooting Hunting Outdoor Tradeshow in Las Vegas, knife maker Gerber sold a knife branded to television adventurer Bear Grylls. The knife sold for $10 and proceeds benefited the Boy Scouts of America.

Columbia Sports Wear and Conservation Alliance

Columbia Sports Wear held six fashion shows at the Outdoor Retailers Show. When trade show attendees tweeted a picture with the hashtag #ORshowCA, CSW made a $5 donation to the Conservation Alliance. See Figure 23.1.

FIGURE 23.1

Columbia Sports Wear Supports Conservation Alliance

BBH Labs Helps Homeless in Austin

At the South by Southwest Interactive Conference in 2012 (SXSWi) BBH Labs launched *Homeless Hotspots* to help Austin's homeless. The company hired homeless men and women to sell "pay what you wish" WiFi service to conference goers. Vendors kept 100 percent of the money they earned. BBH supported the program with a web page that shared the story of each vendor and provided a way for people to donate directly to him or her.

Although the popular media panned *Homeless Hotspots*, homeless advocate and founder of InvisiblePeople.tv, Mark Horvarth, praised the program. "It provides a positive interaction between a homeless vendor and the general public," he said.

Foursquare and Save the Children

At SXSWi in 2010, the location-based service Foursquare teamed up with Microsoft and PayPal to help Save the Children. Every time a conference goer checked in on Foursquare in Austin, Microsoft and PayPal donated 25 cents to Save the Children. The companies capped the donation at $15,000. The program produced 135,000 check-ins.

Purina and Pet Rescue Agencies

At the International Kennel Club Dog Show, pet food giant Purina launched *Rally to Rescue* to support independent pet rescue agencies across the country. For every *Rally to Rescue* sticker signed by attendees and affixed to the wall, Purina made a $1 donation to a local pet organization. Purina even had rescued dogs at the show so attendees could visit with those they supported!

HOW IT WORKS IN 1-2-3

1. Start by identifying trade shows and conferences in your area. You can find a listing on the website of your local convention center, Chamber of Commerce or visitors bureau.

2. Approach the organizers about hosting a fundraiser during the event. Stress the value of doing something creative and enhancing attendee favorability of the event by aligning the conference with a good cause.

3. Work to make your nonprofit's participation in the show or conference just as turnkey as possible. Organizers are busy people and will appreciate a partner that knows how to deliver value.

THINGS TO REMEMBER

- Don't hesitate to call on trade shows in your area. Trade shows are businesses that serve other businesses and consumers. They also have a lot of foot traffic, a key prerequisite for most of the business fundraisers featured in this book.

- Most trade shows have attendees from out of town. Even the conference planners may be visitors. So don't assume that anyone knows about or has even heard of your nonprofit. Be sure to emphasize two of the most important reasons to work with a cause. First, it's what people want. Regardless of the business, people expect them to make the world a better place. Second, they reward businesses that support good causes with their loyalty and favorability. Everyone wins. The company, the consumer, and the cause.

What Nonprofits Can Learn from the Food Trucks outside Trade Shows

I go to a lot of conferences and trade shows, but when I'm hungry I head out to the streets to sample the local food trucks.

I've always been impressed by how food trucks market themselves—especially with social media.

Nonprofits can learn a lot from these mobile eateries that have a nose for where the business is and know how to keep fans coming back.

Their Product is Distinctive

Food trucks are more than just Cokes, hot dogs, and hamburgers. They specialize in delicious, unique, sometimes gourmet food. Consider some of these names of Boston food trucks: Grilled Cheese Nation, Kickass Cupcakes, Bon Me Truck [Vietnamese], Clover Food Truck [vegetarian]. Food trucks have unique offerings and excel within their category. Shouldn't the same be true for nonprofits and the programs they run?

They Adapt

Many food trucks pride themselves on local ingredients, and will change their menus to meet the ebb and flow of the seasons. If something isn't selling, they replace it with something else. If they run out of the something, they improvise. Food trucks know how to turn on a dime! How often can that be said about nonprofits, which steer more like the Titanic than a food truck?

They're People Persons

Food trucks don't wait around for people to come to them. They go where the hungry people are. It might be a college campus or outside a conference or convention center. But too many nonprofits are ivy towers that cut themselves off from the people they can help and the people that can help them. Food trucks are for and by the people. They exist to serve others. So should you.

(continued)

They Have a Cult Like Following

Notice I didn't say that they were good with social media or technology, which they are. Food trucks aren't enamored with tools. But they are focused on what they can accomplish, which is to build a rabid following that looks forward to their tweets and postings and doggedly follows them at every stop. Food trucks thrive because they turn customers into fans and fans into ambassadors. Most importantly, they make it easy to love them. Can you say the same about your nonprofit?

They Understand What's Truly Important

Food trucks succeed or fail for one reason only: their food. It all starts with something that's good, interesting, and a heck of a lot better than your average fast-food joint. Nonprofits need to focus on delivering a product that is superior and valuable. Something that will feed the soul, not fill the gut.

STEAL THESE IDEAS!

1. In 2013, Seattle-based Tisbest released *ExpoGiving*, a fund-raising platform created specifically for trade shows. *ExpoGiving* takes the money that normally goes to trade show tchotchkes and funnels it to charitable organizations that fight hunger, work to end homelessness, conduct medical research, and take environmental action.

2. I attend my share of trade shows and conferences, but I enhance my learning by following the event's hashtag on Twitter. Last year, I followed the happenings at The South by Southwest Interactive Conference in Austin via #SXSWi. I kept seeing tweets from conference goers that said "I ran 4.9 @CharityMiles for @dosomething @nokidhungry." I thought, "What a great idea for attendees to run and support good causes while at the conference!" A smart nonprofit should appeal to conference goers to support their cause while they

are visiting. An even smarter nonprofit would target businesses known for its road warrior employees and introduce them to Charity Miles and its mobile app. You can learn more at CharityMiles.com.

FOR MORE INFORMATION

 You can see more examples of trade show fundraisers by visiting http://fwb40.us/18KkopZ or scan the QR code to view them on your smartphone or tablet.

CHAPTER TWENTY-FOUR

Dress-Down/Up Fundraiser

Dress-down/up fundraisers have been popular for as long as *casual days* or *casual Fridays* have been a trend in North America.

Employees love to escape the corporate dress code and swap their suits and skirts for comfy tees, jeans, and sneakers. Enterprising do-gooders and nonprofits surmised that employees would even pay to dress-down. They were right and a fundraiser was born!

Today, dress-down/up fundraisers are a well-known—if not well-worn—part of corporate America. Let's explore how we can update the style of these fundraisers to fit the needs and practices of a new style-conscious generation.

DRESS-DOWN/UP FUNDRAISERS COME IN ALL HEM LENGTHS AND SHOE SIZES

The most common model for a dress-down fundraiser is a simple casual day that employees donate to participate in. However, nonprofits and businesses have adopted as many variations as there are clothes to wear in the workplace.

The granddaddy of casual days is *Lee's National Denim Day* to support the American Cancer Society. For $5, employees can wear their jeans to work. Since inception, National Denim Day has raised $88 million.

Employees can wear jeans for other causes. The USO, which has supported American troops since 1941, the USO, has *Jeans for GI* days.

FIGURE 24.1

Staff at the Reno-Sparks Convention and Visitors Authority Wear Red in Support of Women's Heart Health Month

Source: Courtesy of RenoTahoe via Flickr.

The Junior Achievement of Chicago encourages employees to sign up for casual days right on the company website. Not only can you pick the day, but you can pay to dress-down for several months.

On National Red Day, supporters of the American Heart Association's (AHA) *Go Red for Women,* can donate to wear their favorite red garment. See Figure 24.1. AHA encourages donors to upload their show of red to the nonprofit's Facebook page. Is red not your color? You can dress in blue on World Water Day.

Boston's Jimmy Fund, the fundraising arm of the Dana-Farber Cancer Institute, has its own red fundraiser, but the colors are found in the hats and shirts of the Boston Red Sox, which employees can wear on opening day for a $5 donation. *Dress for Sox-cess* is a perfect fundraiser for Boston's baseball diehards or for anyone who wants to wear a Red Sox jersey instead of a suit jacket.

Why stop at clothes? TOMS Shoes is asking company partners to wear nothing at all for charity—at least on their feet. *One Day*

Without Shoes encourages people to go shoeless to show their support for shoe donations and the end of hookworm, a soil-transmitted parasite that worldwide affects twice as many people than live in the United States.

Wearing *different* shoes is also an option. The National Association of Basketball Coaches and more than 4,000 college basketball coaches lace up to fight cancer during *Coaches vs. Cancer Suits and Sneakers Weekend*. Instead of suits with shoes, coaches match slacks with pink sneakers to support the American Cancer society.

Casual days for a cause are a fun, easy, creative way for companies to raise money for their favorite charities. The clothes you wear are a great way to show how much you care.

HOW IT WORKS IN 1-2-3

1. Working with your business partner, choose a dress-down/up fundraiser.
2. Promote the event and designate an employee(s) to collect donations.
3. The day of the fundraiser, support the event with incentives and recognition for employees and the organizers.

THINGS TO REMEMBER

- Incentivize and reward employees. Support the fundraiser with t-shirts, wristbands, subs, pizzas, or ice cream donated from a local business. For extra fun, host a raffle.

- Ask the company to donate something special, such as a special parking spot, extra vacation day or company apparel for the employee that shows the most spirit or raises the most money.

- Create a festive atmosphere. Add signs, posters, stickers, or buttons to help promote the event and get employees in the spirit.

Why Companies Don't Care About Your Nonprofit

Companies are less interested in helping your nonprofit than they are in supporting causes that their employees and customers care about.

The latest example is a new initiative from American Honda Motor Company that is working to save America's drive-ins.

The situation is critical. Soon, the movie industry will switch from film to digital. New digital projectors aren't cheap—$80,000—and many family drive-ins will have to close.

Honda is donating five projectors to drive-ins, and the public will choose who gets them in a new contest called *Project Drive-In*.

Honda's efforts to save drive-ins reminds me of another campaign: *Nature Valley Trail View*. Expanding on a long term commitment to this country's national parks, Nature Valley did for hiking trails what Google Street View did for roads: allow people to follow and zoom in on trails in four famous parks.

I think campaigns like Honda's and Nature Valley's are the future of how businesses will support causes.

The Intersection of Cause, Caring and Location

The future of nonprofit and for-profit partnerships is a move away from kitschy pinups and pink-ribbon toasters to deeper connections that drive brand loyalty. Technology is accelerating the evolution of these partnerships and making them omnipresent and, thanks to mobile devices, portable. Nonprofits that aren't building and cultivating strong, emotional brands are more endangered than drive-ins, and less likely to be saved.

The Company Takes a Backseat

Honda created *Project Drive-In*, but the brand is putting a "vanishing American icon" in the driver's seat. The campaign

(continued)

has a unique URL and the Honda logo is not prominently featured. Instead of leading with its name, Honda is driving home the values it shares with consumers.

As a member of the marketing team at Nature Valley explained last year, "Supporting lifestyle causes that your customers care about is what's going to keep them loyal to you, and when they have a choice, maybe they'll choose you."

Every Brand is a Content Creator

Honda is investing in creating online content for the things their customers care for. It's a direction we'll see a lot of companies and nonprofits taking as they look beyond just *adding value* and focus instead on *being valuable*.

Smaller businesses and nonprofits will respond with their own strategies to deepen their connection with causes and customers. Their results won't be as sophisticated as Nature Valley's, but they will blaze their own trail.

Whether you are a large or small business or nonprofit, consumers will expect you to be where they are, to care where they care. Will you make the trip to meet them?

STEAL THESE IDEAS!

1. Ugly Christmas sweater fundraisers are getting more popular every year! Thanks to the latest mobile technology, you can even have a virtual ugly Christmas sweater contest. The *Sweater-izer*, available in Apple's app store for Christmas 2012, let you update a picture of you, a friend or even a favorite celebrity with Christmas and Hanukkah sweaters and festive hats. For a $5 donation to your cause, employees could submit their creations to a contest to pick the best of the worst.

2. What about a dress-down/up fundraiser at a restaurant? To encourage its new dress code, a Southern California restaurant offered to donate 50 percent of every check to the American

Cancer Society if women wore heels. Not to be sexist, if men wore heels 75 percent of their check was donated to ACS!

3. Target companies that have matching gift programs. When employees donate to a dress-down/up the company will double their donation.

4. Encourage employees to form teams with a captain. Have them reach out to friends, family, and other businesses to support their team.

5. Get the company's vendors involved either by supporting the teams or hosting their own dress-down/up fundraiser for your cause.

FOR MORE INFORMATION

 You can see more examples of dress-down/up fund-raisers by visiting http://fwb40.us/17P5JuX or scan the QR code to view them on your smartphone or tablet.

CHAPTER TWENTY-FIVE

Movie Theater Fundraiser

These days people have a lot of choices on where they can spend their time and money for entertainment. But they still love to go to the movies.

More people went to the movies last year than went to theme parks (e.g., Disney World) and sporting events (professional hockey, football, baseball and basketball) *combined*.

Movie theaters are busy places full of people of all ages that are spending lots of money for tickets and treats. That's why your nonprofit should be *showing* at your local theater.

FUNDRAISING GOES TO THE MOVIES

The granddaddy of theater fundraisers is a collection program run by The Jimmy Fund, the fundraising arm of the Dana-Farber Cancer Institute in Boston.

Each summer since 1949, participating movie theaters have shown a Jimmy Fund trailer before the start of a feature film. Afterward, volunteers and theater staff invite patrons to contribute to the Jimmy Fund by passing around collection canisters.

In 2011 alone, the program raised over $600,000.

Another fundraiser showing in 1,000 theaters nationwide is Variety the Children's Charity's 23rd annual Gold Heart Pin.

Each year, Variety partners with a major motion picture studio to design a new Gold Heart pin around a movie or character from that studio.

In 2013, Walt Disney Studios Motion Pictures and Pixar Animation Studios partnered with Variety the Children's Charity to create a pin featuring Mike and Sulley, characters from *Monsters, Inc.* and *Monsters University*.

Proceeds benefit Variety programs that serve children who are disabled and disadvantaged around the world. Since 1991, pin sales worldwide have raised $95 million.

Wehrenberg Theatres, with 15 locations throughout the Midwest, is one of the chains supporting Variety's Gold Pin program. They have an interesting twist on the program that has helped them raise over $100,000 annually.

When moviegoers purchase a gold pin with any concession combo, they receive a free candy bar.

The tie-in with concessions is a smart one. But like any point-of-sale program, the key is the question asked by the cashier: "Would you like to buy a Gold Heart pin for $3 to help a disabled child? Buy it with a concession and you get a candy bar free."

Movie theaters are great places for a fundraiser. They're in every community and have plenty of foot traffic. Is your nonprofit *showing* at your local movie theater? This is one production you don't want to miss!

HOW IT WORKS IN 1-2-3

1. Working with your theater partner, pick a start and end date for your fundraiser.

2. If possible, supply the theater with a short movie trailer that profiles your nonprofit and its work.

3. Tap theater employees or recruit volunteers to collect donations from moviegoers.

THINGS TO REMEMBER

- Make your theater fundraiser as turnkey and successful as possible. Instead of relying on the theater's ushers to collect donations after your trailer, recruit and schedule your own volunteers. Every business is doing more with fewer employees, and supplementing their staff with your volunteers may be just what they need to execute a box office hit for your nonprofit.

- Theaters have dozens of shows a day. Focus your limited resources on blockbuster movies and the busiest shows, which tend to be after 6 P.M. during the week and after noon on weekends.

- Whether you use volunteers or theater employees, incentivize frontline staff with small perks (e.g. t-shirts, gift cards, and pizza or ice cream socials) to motivate them to help and to thank them for their efforts.

- You've probably figured out how theaters make their money: selling expensive candy, popcorn and drinks at concessions. Not everyone knows that most of the money from ticket sales goes to the studios and distribution companies. This makes money from concession sales a sacred cow for theaters. So if you're aiming to get a percentage or portion of sales at the theater (see Chapter 1 for percentage-of-sales programs), focus on concessions not tickets.

Three Ways to Turn Distraction into Support

If I've convinced you in this chapter that a movie theater fundraiser is a good idea, convincing you of the fundraising opportunity of television should be easy.

Although most people only visit a movie theater once a month or so, watching television is a daily habit for tens of millions of Americans. And unlike most moviegoers, TV viewers are watching their favorite programs as they multi-task on their smartphone or tablets.

I'm one of those people! I wrote part of this book at night after my family had gone to bed. It was just me, a slumbering dog, and the television! In addition to writing this book, I answered e-mails, researched blog posts, and repeatedly asked the same question about actors I saw on TV: "Is he
(continued)

(*continued*)

dead?" A quick visit to Wikipedia satisfied my curiosity and I would return to my work.

According to a recent study, my two-screen habit isn't unique. For U.S. users, 86 percent of tablet owners and 88 percent of smartphone users watched TV while using their device at least once during the month. The bottom line is that people are using multiple screens in the evening to enhance their TV time. It's time for us to put this dual screen habits to *good* use.

1. Be a *TV Guide* for Your Supporters

I watch shows all the time that deal with divorce, obesity, heart disease, domestic abuse, alcoholism—and that's just on *The Biggest Loser*! Let your supporters know when their evening television viewing will align with your mission, and give them a place to talk about it on your blog, Facebook, Twitter, Instagram, and so forth.

2. Engage Supporters Off-Hours

A lot of nonprofits post on social media during the day, but then go dark after 6 P.M. Publish content during the evening and at night when people are using mobile devices *and* watching television. But don't give them something to read, give them something to watch. Supporters are relaxing and enjoying themselves. Give them something that complements what they're already doing—and not something that feels like work.

3. Ask for money

If people are buying more products and services on their mobile devices, they can donate on them too. In the past year, 87 percent of people have used their mobile device to make a purchase. Advertisers are awakening to how television and mobile can work together to drive sales.

Nonprofits would be smart to experiment combining TV and mobile because the evidence suggests that when it comes to giving, two screens are better than one.

STEAL THESE IDEAS!

1. Don't limit your fundraisers to movie theaters. Traditional theaters can also host fundraisers. In Boston recently, at a production of the *Book of Mormon*, the actors ended their performance by asking the audience to give to Broadway Cares/Equity Fights AIDS, an industry nonprofit that supports AIDS organizations across the United States. Actors stationed at the exits collected donations. In 2011, Broadway Cares raised over $16 million.

2. Experiment with text giving (Chapter 8) and scan-to-give (Chapter 20) fundraisers following your movie trailer. In a recent awareness tactic called *Frozen Cinema*, a German movie theater and nonprofit teamed up to show moviegoers what it's like to be homeless during the winter. They turned the air conditioning in the movie theater down to the freezing temperatures homeless men and women were enduring right outside the theater's doors. To warm moviegoers, the theater gave them blankets tagged with QR codes, which when scanned with a mobile device took them to a donation page.

3. Movie theaters are busy places with lots of foot traffic. Ask the theater to host a pinup fundraiser (Chapter 15). Cashiers at the box office can ask moviegoers to donate a dollar or two to your cause.

4. Get a business to support your organization by having them buy all the tickets to a show and then you can sell them back to supporters at a higher price. Turn it into a special event with refreshments, entertainment, or a lecture before or after the screening.

5. With more businesses than ever trimming their workforces, volunteers will play a key role in the success of your movie theater fundraiser. Offer incentives to attract and motivate volunteers; t-shirts, bags, movie tickets and other gift certificates will do the trick. Also, enter all your volunteers into a contest for a grand prize (donated, of course!).

FOR MORE INFORMATION

 You can see more examples of movie theater fund-raisers by visiting http://fwb40.us/14D2Uej or scan the QR code to view them on your smartphone or tablet.

CHAPTER TWENTY-SIX

Facebook Contest Fundraiser

No type of charity fundraiser has risen faster than Facebook contests. Five years ago they didn't exist. Today, they're one of the most common vehicles for nonprofit fundraising.

I had my first experience with charity contests way back in 2009 when Virgin America challenged Boston nonprofits to a voting contest. The charity that got the most "votes"—e-mails entered into a special contest page—won $25,000. We competed against 400 Boston nonprofits and finished second. Unfortunately, there was no cash prize for the runner-up.

The nonprofit that won was a small Jewish chabad that already had the skills and assets smart nonprofits are still using to win online contests: a strong community of supporters and social media prowess.

With the help of this chapter you may hear the word I never heard in the same sentence with *contest*: winner.

FACEBOOK CONTEST LESSONS FROM TWO WINNERS

Being a charity contest loser, I needed to find a winner. Luckily, I found two: Sandra Morris and John Haydon.

Sandra Morris is co-founder and CEO of CafeGive (www .cafegive.com), a company that specializes in social apps for cause marketing, particularly Facebook apps for nonprofits contests.

John Haydon is a social media expert for nonprofits and author of *Facebook Marketing For Dummies* (www.johnhaydon.com).

Both Sandra and John are Facebook contest experts!

"The number one question nonprofits have about charity contests is how to get started," said John. "You should use a third-party app. Once people see your app (after liking a page), they can then enter the contest via the app."

John recommends a contest app available at Shortstack (www .shortstack.com). He also suggests that you ask for an email address from Facebook users to participate in a contest.

"E-mail is the bridge that takes people from engaging with you on Facebook to donating to your organization," said John.

Sandra's company, CafeGive, offers more consultative solutions for organizations that want to ensure their contest is a winner.

Regardless of which company or service you choose, building a Facebook contest app doesn't have to be expensive.

"There's an account fee and a monthly fee. But most charity contests only run for a couple months," said Sandra. "It's well within the reach of even the smallest organizations."

As an example, Sandra points to Portland Nursery, a single location nursery in Oregon, which worked with CafeGive on a photo contest to support their annual apple tasting event. See Figure 26.1.

The winning photographers received $100 from Portland Nursery and got to choose a local charity to receive a $600 donation from a corporate sponsor. Although the Nursery suggested charities, the winning photographers could choose one of their own.

Over 100 photographers signed up for the contest and submitted their photos for five different categories.

A small committee of judges selected the 15 photos, 3 in each category, to compete in the online contest. The contest was launched as a Facebook tab on the Portland Nursery Facebook page.

To drive voting, the campaign was promoted via email and social media.

After liking the page, visitors could vote in each category, see a summary of results for each photo and share the contest with friends.

Portland Nursery increased their fan base by 500 from the local community to their contest page in less than 15 days, representing over a 30 percent increase. Five local photographers won $100 and directed their sponsored awards to the following local charities: Portland Youth Builders, Village Gardens, and the Oregon Humane Society.

PORTLAND NURSERY PHOTO CONTEST

Vote for one photo in each category below. Winners will be announced October 30, 2011. Each winner will receive a $100 Portland Nursery gift certificate and will select a charity to receive a $600 donation from Whitney Farms.

LIKE
Click **Like** and help us select the winner of our photo competition.

VIEW
View all the photos and select your favorite in each category.

VOTE!
Vote for your 5 picks by clicking here

>>> SUBMIT NOW <<<

or at the bottom of the page.

4,247 people like this. Be the first of your friends.

If you've already liked us, thank you!
click here to view and vote>>

FIGURE 26.1

Portland Nursery's Photo Contest for a Cause

Source: Courtesy of CafeGive.com.

The nursery has made the photo contest an annual event!

HOW IT WORKS IN 1-2-3

1. Choose from three popular Facebook charity contests: A photo contest, a voting contest, or a "Like" (or share) contest.

2. Decide on the donation level for the contest and how long it will run.

3. Promote, promote, promote! See tips below.

THINGS TO REMEMBER

- If you're not using a contest specialist like CafeGive, review Facebook's terms for contests and promotions. They change regularly.

- Dress for success. Your Facebook contest will benefit from graphics that look professional. This isn't hard if you know Illustrator, Photoshop, and so forth. But if you don't, invest in someone who does.

- To succeed with a social media contest you need to be on social media! Charity contests aren't for organizations that are still trying to "figure out" Facebook.

- Get everyone involved, especially employees. They can lead the charge for getting the word out.

- You need to carefully plan your outreach strategy to supporters. You'll need your best supporters to win, but they'll be bombarded with messages and requests to act. Will they be pumped or miffed? You have to engage without alienating.

Facebook Contest Do's and Don't's

John Haydon frequently works with nonprofits on Facebook contests. He has a message for all nonprofits: *Stop begging*.

"Your non-profit rocks and deserves to win," said John. "You're doing great work. Act like this contest is yours to win.

"If you don't think your nonprofit deserves to win you shouldn't be having [a contest] or enter[ing] into a contest."

John is a passionate guy, and getting him started on Facebook contests and nonprofits was like opening a levee!

- **Don't be reactive.** If you've scrambled to jump on this opportunity because you only found out about it last week, then stop. Scrambling is a symptom, but it isn't a good strategy. Winning a contest is the least of your challenges.

- **Do focus on the issue, not on your nonprofit.** People want to take action to end hunger or child abuse; they don't want to help your nonprofit pay salaries and bills.

(*continued*)

- **Don't burn bridges.** Asking for a vote from supporters that aren't ready for a contest could ruin your chances of ever getting more than a vote from them. It's not worth it.

- **Do focus on getting your best supporters to vote.** No—go one step further. Create platforms for them to campaign on your behalf (Facebook Groups, Twitter campaign pages, blogs).

- **Don't lead from behind.** You're the best. That's why people should vote for you. Begging isn't an option. Lead from the front with strength and let the votes fall where they will!

- **Do give them a reason.** Be very clear about what the winning nonprofit gets. Tell them why it matters. *Tip:* a compelling video with music, images, and text telling people why winning matters will inspire people to act.

STEAL THESE IDEAS!

1. For promotion, approach your contest in three phases: launch, dip, and peak. According to Sandra Morris, for a two-month contest you need to plan for a strong kick-off. This means using every communication vehicle you have to get the word out. Like any campaign, there's a natural dip in interest and engagement that you need to counter with powerful stories and short-term goals to keep people motivated and engaged. As you approach the end of the contest, have a plan to get all hands rowing to propel you across the finish line. Plan and execute!

2. Can you host a contest someplace besides Facebook? The short answer is yes, but Facebook contest apps and a huge audience make it a natural winner. Here are three alternatives to Facebook.

   - *On a Blog:* If you or your business partner has an active blog, you can use the comments section for a contest. I saw a business do this with charity bracelets. They posted pictures of the bracelets and asked readers to leave comments on which bracelet they liked the best. The reader's comment that got the most "likes" won the prize.

- *On Twitter:* Hashtags are the key here. In 2010, *USA Today* launched a four-day Twitter hashtag campaign for charity. The grand prize was a full-page, full-color ad in *USA Today*, valued at $189,400. The charity that had the most re-tweets of the message *"#AmericanWants [charity name] to get a full-page ad in USA TODAY"* was declared the winner.

- *On Pinterest:* In a Pinterest contest, users are asked to either upload a photo to a board or repin a photo from an existing board. For example, over the holidays Sony launched a "pin it to give it" contest that donated a dollar to The Michael Phelps Foundation for every re-pin from a Sony products board.

Which platform is the right one for you? It's the one you're already using to engage supporters. Build on what you're already doing well and always go where the people are!

3. John Haydon suggests you get the best prize(s) you can from your corporate partner. People want to help, but prizes entice them to act. John also suggests you follow up quickly with contest participants about supporting your organization. "In a Facebook contest I did with a pet shelter in New Hampshire, 50 percent of participants donated to the shelter after we followed up with them by e-mail," said John. "Participating in a contest (in this case a pet photo) means people are interested in your organization. Ask them for money!"

FOR MORE INFORMATION

 You can see more examples of Facebook contest fundraisers by visiting http://fwb40.us/19xgLGb or scan the QR code to view them on your smartphone or tablet.

CHAPTER TWENTY-SEVEN

Donate-Profits Day Fundraiser

We've all heard the Latin expression *carpe diem*, which means, "seize the day." But in fundraising with businesses, a new expression is taking hold: "da die," which is Latin for "give the day."

Here's how it works. Generous businesses support nonprofits by donating the profits from one day's sales.

Unlike a percentage of sales fundraiser (Chapter 1) that donates a percentage or portion of sales from every product or service sold for a day, week, or month, and so forth, donate-profits days are a percentage of the day's total receipts.

This fundraiser has its merits because it forces both business and nonprofit to focus their efforts around a single day, and to potentially raise a lot of money!

FOUR BUSINESSES THAT ARE GIVING THE DAY

Whole Foods Markets and One Fund Boston

Shortly after the Boston Marathon bombing, Whole Foods Markets in New England hosted a Community Giving Day (a.k.a donate-profits day) to support the victims. Five percent of the net sales from the day went to the One Fund Boston, the fund created by the Mayor of Boston and Governor of Massachusetts to support the bombing victims. See Figure 27.1.

It wasn't the first time Whole Foods had hosted a donate-profits days. Whole Food stores across the country have giving days four times a year. These giving days support local causes, such as the

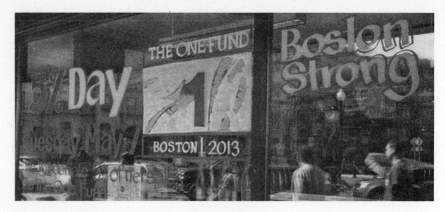

FIGURE 27.1

This Supermarket Plans to Donate 5 Percent of the Day's Profits to Charity

YMCA, Boys & Girls Clubs, and other health, environmental, and education nonprofits.

At my local Whole Foods just outside Boston, nonprofits are encouraged to set up a display and have staff on hand to educate shoppers about their work.

Chili's Grill & Bar and St. Jude Children's Research Hospital

As part of its annual fundraising effort for St. Jude Children's Research Hospital, restaurant chain Chili's Grill & Bar donates 100 percent of the profits on its donate-profits day.

In the days before and after the donate-profits day, Chili's sells *Create-a-Pepper* coloring sheets to raise additional funds. This past year, Chili's added a QR code to coloring sheets so diners could donate via their mobile devices. Although numbers were not released on how much was raised, we do know that consumers scanned the QR Codes nearly 300,000 times.

Kansas City Restaurants and Good Samaritan Project

Every April, more than two dozen Kansas City restaurants team up to raise money for Kansas City's Good Samaritan Project, the community's oldest AIDS service organization.

Supporters of the fundraiser range from large restaurant chains to mom and pop diners to breakfast joints and upscale restaurants. What they all have in common is that they've pledged at least 25 percent of the day's gross to the Good Sam Project.

"This is the third year that we've done this event in Kansas City," says C. Aaron Nickless, manager of development and marketing for the Good Samaritan Project. "In 2011 we started with six participating restaurants. Last year we had over 20 restaurants. We've raised $50,000 so far."

Massage Envy and Arthritis Foundation

As part of its annual drive for *Healing Hands with Arthritis*, Massage Envy picks a day in September to donate $10 from every massage and facial to the Arthritis Foundation.

Massage Envy shows how you can add a twist to donate-profits day by limiting the donation to one or two products. Although donate-profits day is a variation of percentage-of-sales fundraisers (see Chapter 1), they are different in that donate-profits day is limited to one day but the donation is based on total sales.

HOW IT WORKS IN 1-2-3

1. Working with your business partner, choose a day for your donate-profits day.

2. In advance of the event, promote the fundraiser to the company's customers and to your supporters.

3. On the donate-profits day, have fun with it! Create a display to inform customers of the fundraiser, and have staff and a client on hand to tell your nonprofit's story.

THINGS TO REMEMBER

- Be clear with your business partner on what donate-profits day means to them. Will it be all profits, or will they donate a percentage or portion of profits? For example, on its

Community Giving Days, Whole Foods Market donates 5 percent of net sales.

- Donate-profits day can be limited to a certain product or section within a business. For example, Whole Foods Market hosted *Salad Bar Donation Day*. For every purchase from a salad bar at stores nationwide, the company donated 5 percent of the day's net sales to Whole Kids Foundation to support salad bar grants for schools across the country.

- The worst thing a business owner can hear a customer say on a donate-profits day is "I had no idea that was happening here today." It's deflating for the business because they hadn't planned to give the money anonymously. It's your nonprofit's responsibility to make sure that every customer knows the business is doing a *good thing* that day. Customers shouldn't have to search for it!

Four Mistakes You Don't Have to Make

Mistakes are part of life. I certainly have made my share! Here are four mistakes you don't have to make when fundraising with businesses.

1. Wasting your time coming up with creative ideas when partnerships are the key to success

I love interesting fundraising ideas. That's why I wrote this book! But these brilliant ideas are nothing without a business partner to execute them. Given the choice between a novel fundraising idea and a business partner interested in a simple fundraiser, such as pinups or donations boxes, I'll take the latter any day.

2. Assuming that every company wants to be your life-long partner

Business partners are like friends. Some are good, life-long friends and others are the fair-weather kind. Don't confuse the

(continued)

two. Some partners will stick with you for a year or two and then they'll move on to something else, maybe another non-profit. Although friends are great, you should never stop making new ones.

3. Being unhappy with just making money

Nonprofits need to be realistic about what a business fundraiser can accomplish. Yes, it can increase awareness of your cause. Yes, it can deepen a relationship with an existing partner. But one of the best things about fundraising with businesses is the money. Cash is tangible, measurable, and the fuel that will feed your mission.

4. Growing too big, too fast

Any nonprofit can raise money with businesses. But don't go too fast or commit too many resources to the effort. Grow your program organically and commit resources as needed. Not every cause is the next St. Jude Children's Research Hospital or Product RED. Most causes are destined to do just one or two fundraisers a year.

For 9 out of 10 nonprofits, fundraising with businesses will be transactional, sporadic, and uncertain. I'm obviously a big fan of raising money with businesses. But nonprofits need be realistic and honest about their potential. Any truth is better than make believe.

STEAL THESE IDEAS!

1. Any type of business can participate in donate-profits days. Take BTIG LLC, a global financial services firm, which annually hosts *Commissions for Charity Day*. My pick of industries to host a donate-profits day is the oil industry. Daily, they make hundreds of millions of dollars in profits. I say seize the day and give the day!

2. Take your cue from Chili's and St. Jude and add other fund-raising efforts that culminate in a donate-profits days (e.g. Pinups, donation boxes, scan-to-give, percentage-of-sales or cause product).

3. A day of giving doesn't have to be all about money. Heineken USA kicked off its annual conference with attendees donating a day of work to the Give Kids the World Village, a nonprofit resort in Kissimmee, Florida. Volunteers tackled projects like painting, landscaping, cleaning venues, and sanitizing toys, which will help to provide a safer and more pleasant retreat for visiting families.

FOR MORE INFORMATION

 You can see more examples of donate-profits day fundraisers by visiting http://fwb40.us/14D6V24 or scan the QR code to view them on your smartphone or tablet.

CHAPTER TWENTY-EIGHT

Buy One Give One Fundraiser

It's not a stretch to say that TOM's Shoes has popularized *buy one, give one* (BOGO) as much as Starbucks has popularized corner coffee shops.

When you think of BOGO you think of TOM's, which was started by Blake Mycoskie in 2006. The name says it all. When you buy a pair of shoes from TOM's, they donate a new pair to a child in need. In 2010 the company celebrated giving away 1 million shoes.

A lot of organizations have followed TOM's lead and launched BOGO programs. They range from full-fledged cause businesses that incorporate BOGO into their business practices to traditional businesses that run BOGO promotions. In this chapter we'll look at both.

SEVEN BUSINESSES THAT GIVE ONE EVERY TIME THEY SELL ONE

People Water

People Water is a for-profit, cause-based business that is committed to alleviating the global water crisis. For every purchase of its bottled spring water, People Water gives an equal amount of clean water to people in need.

Harry's

Founded by Warby Parker, which donates a pair of eyeglasses for every one sold, Harry's proposes to do the same for shaving gear.

For every pack of Harry's blades you buy, they donate one blade to an organization that supports its mission of helping people to look and feel great.

Maggiano Little Italy

For one month, Maggiano's restaurants make a meal donation to Feeding America for every Classic Pasta ordered in October. But Maggiano's has added its own spin to BOGO. For every order of Classic Pasta ordered, diners get a free order to bring home. They call the program *Buy-One, Take-One, Give-One*.

The Company Store

As a company known for its bedding, The Company Store donates a comforter to a homeless child for every comforter purchased. The comforter is a "blankie" for children that they can bring with them from the shelter to a permanent home.

Two Degrees

For every gluten-free, vegan bar that shoppers buy, Two Degrees gives a meal to a hungry child. Last year, they sold and gave away over 200,000 bars.

Smiles for the People

Smiles for the People takes a slightly different approach to buy one, give one, which they explain on their website.

"Some 'One for One' companies give away one physical product for every one you buy, but to be most effective, we do it differently. Instead of giving away physical toothbrushes, *our Giving Partners tell us exactly what they need*. They might ask us for the funds to open a new clinic, buy supplies, run a training program, or facilitate community outreach and education. And yes, they may sometimes even need a donation of toothbrushes."

Better World Books

Better World Books believes that education and access to books are basic human rights. That's why books sold on its website support high-impact literacy projects in the United States and around the world. They match every purchase on their website with a book donation to someone in need—book for book.

HOW IT WORKS IN 1-2-3

1. Working with your business partner, identify an item that, when purchased, will trigger the donation of an exact or similar item to your organization.

2. Set a start and end date for the promotion, and set a limit on how many items will be donated.

3. Determine how and when you'll receive the donated item (e.g. before the program, weekly, at the end).

THINGS TO REMEMBER

- Your goal isn't to convince your business partner to become the next TOM's Shoes. Far from it. You just want them to give your organization a product or service whenever a customer buys one. We don't necessarily need more BOGO businesses. But we do need more businesses that are inspired by them!

- Don't agree to a BOGO promotion if you don't really need the donated item, or if you can't handle a large shipment of something you do need. Agreeing to a BOGO promotion just so you can start a relationship with a business—I've seen it before—is shortsighted, selfish, and wasteful.

- There's no one way to use BOGO. The customer's purchase can trigger the donation of the same product, a different product, or cash.

The Role of Emotion in Fundraising with Businesses

Emotion is important for all types of fundraising, including fundraising with businesses. If a cashier asks a shopper to make a donation to UNICEF's Tap Project because "1 in 10 watersheds in this country are polluted," the shopper will shrug and move on. But if the cashier asks for a gift so "our children can have clean, safe tap water to drink," more shoppers will give.

Recently in a department store a cashier held up a sneaker-shaped pinup and asked me to donate to the Juvenile Diabetes Research Foundation. I gave, as I always do, but I bet a lot of shoppers didn't. The cashier would have gotten a better response from shoppers if she led with a question that mentioned the children JDRF helps: "You probably know someone with diabetes. I know I do. We're raising money today for children with the disease. Can we count on your support?"

Still, asking shoppers to support Juvenile Diabetes Research Foundation isn't a bad fundraising pitch.

Large nonprofits can usually rely on their household names at the register because they've been soaked in emotion for decades (e.g., Komen for the Cure [breast cancer], Salvation Army [kettle bells for the poor and disaster relief], children's hospitals [sick kids]). Certain nonprofit brands trigger feelings as soon as we see, hear, or come into contact with them.

But most nonprofits have poor name and brand recognition. Instead of their names they should lead with their strongest emotional message: children instead of adults, puppies instead of animals, community gardens instead of farms. Play your strongest card first. Of course, nonprofits worry that . . .

Leaving their name out will hurt their cause. Is promoting a name that no one knows better? When I worked at a Boston hospital with low brand awareness we led with emotion. "Would you like to donate a dollar to help a poor,

(continued)

sick child?" If moved, shoppers got a takeaway about our organization so they could learn more about what they just gave to.

Focusing on one emotional issue is lying and damaging to their cause. When I suggest leading with emotion, nonprofits respond that it doesn't capture the breadth of their mission (e.g., asking a local animal group to focus on puppies when they help all kinds of animals from cats to birds to reptiles). Your emotional lead is like a vanguard—your best force that will lead your nonprofit forward. Slicing through consumer apathy and indecision, it turns the former into interest and the latter into resolve.

A great example of a nonprofit driving with emotion is The Jimmy Fund, the fundraising arm of Boston's Dana-Farber Cancer Institute. Although the mission of The Jimmy Fund is to raise money to fight adult and pediatric cancers, their cause marketing campaigns lead with emotion: sick kids with cancer.

Choosing a truly sad appeal will turn shoppers off. Think again. Fundraising expert Jeff Brooks makes the case for sad faces.

People are more sympathetic and give more to a charity when the victim portrayed on the advertisement expressed sadness than when a victim expressed happiness or neutral emotion . . . . The authors illustrate when and how a sad expression enhances sympathy and giving. Taken together, the findings imply the importance of subtle emotional cues that sway sympathy and giving.

Research is great, but as Jeff explains, experienced fundraisers know without asking: A sad face gets a better response.

Although nonprofits need to balance emotion with rational arguments, and avoid appeals that are too severe or prolonged, emotion is a critical element for cause marketing success.

Ignore emotion at your own peril. Without it, consumers just might leave your cause at the register with the rest of the things they decided not to buy.

STEAL THESE IDEAS!

1. An offshoot of BOGO is *Paying It Forward*, that is, when businesses allow consumers to pay one forward for someone more needy. For example, Starbucks in the United Kingdom allows customers to purchase *suspended coffee* for the homeless. Starbucks matches the customer's donation with its own cash gift to a charity. Inspired by stories of generous citizens who anonymously paid the balance of layaway orders, Toys "R" Us donated $200 worth of toys to Toys for Tots each time it happened in a store during the holidays. Think of all the different types of businesses that could encourage customers to pay it forward and support your mission. Buy one for yourself and one for someone in need!

FOR MORE INFORMATION

 You can see more examples of buy one give one fundraisers by visiting http://fwb40.us/1ak5iLe or scan the QR code to view them on your smartphone or tablet. Additionally, I have a Pinterest board specifically for *Pay It Forward* fundraisers. You can view it at http://fwb40.us/fwbpif.

CHAPTER TWENTY-NINE

Matching Gifts

If we asked a random group of people to name a popular corporate giving program, most of them would answer "matching gifts". They've been around since General Electric launched the first program in 1954.

Matching gifts are *free* company money that "match" an employee donation to a qualified nonprofit. An employee donation of $25 becomes $50, and so forth.

As the name suggests, matching gifts double a donation, but guidelines vary depending on the company (Some companies offer an even more generous "match". For example, New York-based Soros Management Fund, offers a whopping 3:1 match.).

Regardless of how much the company match is, matching gifts are good for everyone. The nonprofit raises more money. The employee feels supported by her employer. And the employer has an engaged employee that's a positive ambassador in the community.

NONPROFITS CAN DOUBLE THEIR PLEASURE WITH MATCHING GIFTS

John Wright spends his workdays helping his clients make good matches.

No, John isn't a professional matchmaker for men and women in search of fun and love. He's a business-development director for HEP Development, a Virginia-based company that's a leader in providing nonprofits with the tools they need to take advantage of corporate matching gift opportunities.

John shared a few facts about matching gifts that are sure to capture your interest in this popular but often undervalued corporate giving program.

- 1 in 10 gifts is matchable.
- Around half of Corporate 500 Companies offer matching gifts.
- HEP Development is adding a new matching company to its database daily.

Smart nonprofits that have doubled their efforts to tap matching gift programs are reaping the rewards. The American Cancer Society quadrupled what they raised in three years from $2 million to $10 million.

Do I have your attention now? Good. Here's what John suggests to have your own successful matching gift program.

"First, your organization has to be 100 percent committed to finding and securing matching gifts," said John. "All the key players in your organization have to be convinced of the benefits and committed to a successful program."

If your organization is large, you may want to entrust the program to several key team members. However, even if your nonprofit is small, the program should still have a champion to ask, "Are we making the most of this fundraiser as a matching gift opportunity?"

"Next, it's important that you use every resource you have to collect information on donors' employers," explained John. "If you don't know where a donor works you can't find out if they have a matching gift program."

The key is to make the box for "employer" as required as name, address, and credit card number on all donor communications. If a donor forgot to include her address when making a gift, would you ask her for it? Be sure to give employer information the same priority.

"Finally, promotion is key," said John. "'Does your employer have a matching gift program?' has to be on the lips of every employee, volunteer and donor."

You can put a matching gift tab on your website. And don't forget to include the information in brochures, thank you letters, newsletters, and online fundraising sites. Don't give people an excuse to forget or to say no.

"Nonprofits know that money doesn't grow on trees," said John. "But money from corporate matching gifts may be the closest thing to it."

HOW IT WORKS IN 1-2-3

1. The nonprofit shares the matching-gift information with donors.

2. The nonprofit receives the matching-gift form from the donor and fills out the required information.

3. The nonprofit verifies the donation and submits the form back to the company.

THINGS TO REMEMBER

- With some companies offering a 2:1 match or more, it's easy to think that promoting a 1:1 match may not get donors' attention. Think again. Research shows that *size* of the match doesn't matter. Donors offered a one-to-one match gave just as often, and just as much, as those responding to more generous matches.

- Talking about matching gifts is boring. Talking about the impact they can have on your organization isn't. Show people what matching gifts have done for your organization. That's why promoting your program on social networks such as Facebook, where you can post pictures and videos, is so powerful.

- Research shows that when trying to fund a specific program or project with matching gifts, it helps to show donors that you've already raised a good portion of the money. In short, if you want to be successful with matching gifts, start by soliciting seed money to fund your program or project and watch your matches grow!

- Many companies match donations up to a year after an employee makes a donation. So it may not be too late to revisit the company and double the gift!

Ten Tips for Matching Gift Success

1. Make it as easy as possible for donors to have their gift matched. Break down the gift process and identify opportunities to promote matching gifts.

2. When donors are submitting donations online, require that they include "employer" information.

3. Identify the top matching-gift employers in your area and make sure everyone on your team is aware of them and the potential revenue. Keep this information updated to note changes and opportunities.

4. Subscribe to a service such as Double the Donation (www.doublethedonation.com) or HEP Development (www.hepdata.com) where you can check matching-gift eligibility, review program guidelines, and gain access to the forms needed to submit their matching-gift request.

5. Share success stories with your donors in your newsletter, website, and thank-you letters. Show them the potential of matching gifts and how it's *free* money just waiting to be claimed.

6. Make an extra effort to thank donors that submit their matching-gift paperwork and take advantage of their employer's program.

7. Educate your major gifts team on matching-gift programs that have a high maximum match. For
(continued)

example, Microsoft matches employee donations up to $12,000.

8. Social media is a great way to remind supporters of matching gifts and the potential revenue for your organization.

9. Set a goal for matching gifts for your nonprofit and put activities and resources in place to achieve it.

10. Develop a matching-gift management system to keep track of gifts and the status of the matching-gift submission and collection.

STEAL THESE IDEAS!

1. Your nonprofit can comb company websites looking for matching gift program information, or subscribe to a database for this information. But you can also "borrow" the database on another nonprofit's website. For example, my alma mater, Penn State University, has a search bar on its giving page that allows me to search for companies that have a matching-gift program. Find your own database by searching Google for "Which companies match donations?"

2. Upgrade your promotional materials for your matching gift program every couple of years. Linda Stark, Matching Gifts Specialist in the Advancement Services office at California Polytechnic State University, told HEP Development how it works. "If we send out the same slip for three years, people are eventually going to stop looking at it. If we change the look on a regular basis, it will continue to look fresh and appealing."

3. Add an event component to your matching-gift program. For example, as part of the exclusive *Believe in Reading* partnership with Justin Bieber, Barnes & Noble/NOOK matched all donations by student fundraisers up to $50,000. The

grand-prize-winning middle or high school received a visit from Bieber. You don't need an event with Justin Bieber to be successful. But you do need a company that will match the donations made to your run, walk, ride, gala, dress-down, or whatever event.

4. Companies don't need a formal matching-gift program to match gifts. They also can match gifts from anyone—and not just from employees. For example, to celebrate the 60th anniversary of the partnership between the Boston Red Sox and The Jimmy Fund at Dana-Farber Cancer Institute, the Red Sox issued a challenge match. Beginning on opening day in 2013, they offered to match gifts to the Jimmy Fund up to $60,000. After the Boston Marathon bombing a local super-market chain, Shaw's, asked their customers to donate at the register to support the victims. In addition to their own generous donation, Shaw's matched customer donations up to $100,000. See Figure 29.1.

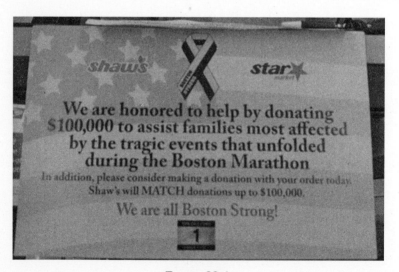

FIGURE 29.1

This Boston Supermarket Chain Matched Donations from Customers up to $100,000

FOR MORE INFORMATION

 You can see more examples of matching gift programs by visiting http://fwb40.us/18P5S0k or scan the QR code to view them on your smartphone or tablet.

CHAPTER THIRTY

Round-up Fundraiser

Round-up fundraisers are similar to pinups (Chapter 15) in that the cashier asks the customer to support a nonprofit. But there's no paper icon and the suggested donation isn't $1 to $5. Instead, shoppers are asked to "round-up" to the nearest dollar on their purchases.

Businesses aren't stopping with round-up programs in brick and mortar businesses. Online programs—fundraisers that ask shoppers to give when they make purchases online—are gaining popularity with e-tailers that are eager to extend online shopping to online giving.

J. C. PENNEY SUPPORTS CHARITIES
WITH ROUND-UP AT CHECKOUT

One retailer that has made round-ups a priority is department store chain J. C. Penney. They're currently using round-ups both in store and at jcpenney.com to raise money for a different charity every month.

Some of the benefiting organizations include The Salvation Army, Dress for Success, and Share Our Strength.

Since J.C. Penney launched the round-up program as part of *jcpcares* in July 2012, it's raised over $1 million per month. Although the average round-up is just 44 cents, shopper participation has been high. Picking the right charities to support has helped the round-up program.

"We really try to pick charities that are relevant to the month," explained Miki Woodard, J. C. Penney's vice president of philanthropy. "When we launched the program July 1st we chose the USO in support of our troops. In December, we supported The Salvation Army."

J. C. Penney supports their round-up program with additional fundraising. Their support for the USO included a donation for every check-in on Foursquare. The retailer invited The Salvation Army to set up their red kettles outside Penney stores. Lastly, during the month that they supported the National 4-H Council, they donated a dollar from every haircut in their salons.

Beginning in 2013, J. C. Penney began accepting online round-ups at checkout at www.jcpenney.com. See Figure 30.1.

HOW IT WORKS IN 1-2-3

1. Your business partner agrees to host a round-up at their business or online on their website.

2. Work with the business to determine how the donation will be recorded by their offline and/or online point-of-sale system.

3. Decide on the duration of the program (generally two to four weeks), educate employees, and execute the program.

THINGS TO REMEMBER

- The cashier asking for a customer to round-up is critical for the program's success. Unlike pinups, there is no paper icon to catch the shopper's eye or curiosity. If the cashier doesn't ask, there will be no donation.

- The lure of round-up programs is you're asking people for nothing more than their extra change. It's an easy yes. That's why it helps if the cashier highlights how much they'll be donating. "Your total today is $17.51. We're hosting a fundraiser for the local women's shelter. Would you like to round-up and donate 49 cents?" It's that easy!

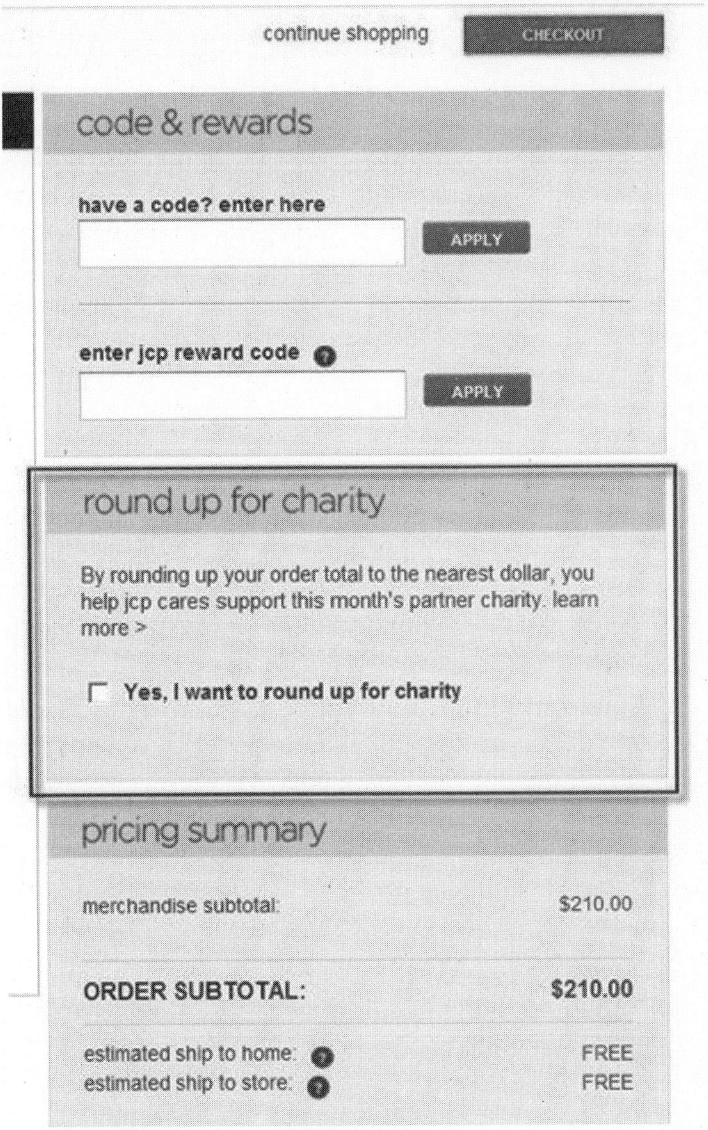

continue shopping   CHECKOUT

code & rewards

have a code? enter here

APPLY

enter jcp reward code ❓

APPLY

round up for charity

By rounding up your order total to the nearest dollar, you help jcp cares support this month's partner charity. learn more >

☐ **Yes, I want to round up for charity**

pricing summary

merchandise subtotal:	$210.00
ORDER SUBTOTAL:	**$210.00**
estimated ship to home: ❓	FREE
estimated ship to store: ❓	FREE

FIGURE 30.1

J. C. Penney's Online Round-Up Program

Source: Courtesy of J. C. Penney.

Three Reasons Why Round-up Programs Are the Best Kind of Point of Sale Fundraiser

Register programs (Chapter 2), pinups (Chapter 15), donation boxes (Chapter 3) and round-ups fall under what I call *point of sale programs* (or POS, not to be confused with the *percentage of sale* programs I discuss in Chapter 1).

All four programs happen at checkout when the cashier is interacting with the customer and processing payment.

Which one is the best? I have to go with the round-up. Here's why.

1. **Round-ups aren't passive.** Round-ups begin with a request from the cashier: "Do you want to round-up your purchase to the nearest dollar to help children with cancer?" Just like at McDonald's when the cashier asks you if you want to supersize your meal, a question asked by the cashier works!

2. **Round-ups raise more money.** I don't have research to back up my claim, but I think when someone asks you to donate less than a buck it's easy to say yes. I've seen pin-up programs ask for as much as $5, but fewer people will say yes. A round-up is an easy yes. Remember, J. C. Penney is raising over $1 million a month with an average round-up of just 44 cents. That's a lot of people saying yes.

3. **Round-ups are easy to execute.** No donation boxes. No coin counting. No paper-waste pin-ups. No need for posters, pins, or register signs. The cashier handles the entire transaction from ask to thank you.

Round-up programs are lucrative, inexpensive, and efficient. They're the perfect POS fundraiser!

STEAL THESE IDEAS!

1. Train cashiers to capitalize on customer enthusiasm for rounding up by encouraging willing customers to make an additional donation of any amount.

2. GoDaddy.com, a domain registrar and web hosting company, encourages customers to round-up at checkout and gives them three charities to support. They also match the customer's donation. So, that 75-cent donation from your round-up is doubled to $1.50. Giving people a choice of charities to support and doubling their donation are incentives to give! You can also offer them a discount, deal, or special after they round-up.

FOR MORE INFORMATION

 You can see more examples of round-up fundraisers by visiting http://fwb40.us/17L8Juc or scan the QR code to view them on your smartphone or tablet.

CHAPTER THIRTY-ONE

In-Store Fundraiser

In-store fundraisers share a strong connection with collection drives (Chapter 22), pinups (Chapter 15), actions-triggered donations (Chapter 6) and other fundraisers highlighted in this book. These, too, happen in the store. But the in-store fundraisers profiled in this chapter have a strong promotional element because they're focused on filling the store with customers.

One of my favorite in-store fundraisers, which I also discuss in Chapter 11 on company giveaways, is IHOP's free pancakes day.

Since 2006, IHOP has picked a day to give away a free short stack of buttermilk pancakes at its 1,500 restaurants. In return, IHOP asks customers to donate to the Children's Miracle Network. Since inception, the program has raised over $10 million.

These special promotions are meant to drive support to CMN and traffic into IHOP locations. In-store fundraisers are potent one-day events that are fun, high energy, and creative. I say pass the syrup.

PUMA RUNS WICKED GOOD IN-STORE FUNDRAISER

Patriots Day in my home state of Massachusetts officially commemorates the start of the American Revolutionary War in Lexington and Concord, Massachusetts.

However, it's also *Marathon Monday* and the running of the most famous road race in the world: the Boston Marathon (okay, I'm biased).

Marathon day always brings its share of fun and interesting marketing promotions as companies vie for the attention of the estimated half-million spectators that line the marathon course.

In 2011, footwear and apparel maker, PUMA, staged an in-store fundraiser to support Soles4Souls, a charity that provides shoes to poor people around the world.

For three days, including Marathon Monday, runners lined up at PUMA's Boston store location to run on a treadmill set-up in the store's front display window. For each mile recorded on the in-store treadmill, PUMA donated $100 and a pair of shoes to Soles4Souls. See Figure 31.1. The fundraiser generated plenty of money and shoes for Soles4Souls and a lot of interest and traffic for the PUMA store.

Here's the good news: you don't have to be an international footwear brand to execute a program like this. It's a simple in-store promotion that anyone who wants to help a good cause by having a *good run* can do!

FIGURE 31.1

A Runner Supports Soles4Souls at PUMA's Boston Store

HOW IT WORKS IN 1-2-3

1. The business partner agrees to host a fundraising event in its stores from which your nonprofit will receive a portion or percentage of the total sales from purchases that day. The fundraiser can also be action-triggered like PUMA's fundraiser.

2. The nonprofit and the business promote the fundraiser to their supporters and customers.

3. The day of the event, the business tracks actions or purchases and donates a percentage of the total sales, or a portion of the sales from specific customers (e.g., shoppers who identify themselves as supporters of your nonprofit), to your nonprofit.

THINGS TO REMEMBER

- In-store fundraisers work well with special occasions (review Chapter 37). PUMA's in-store fundraiser tied in nicely with the Boston Marathon when racers and spectators were clogging Boston's downtown streets. IHOP's free pancake day happens on *National Pancake Day* and benefits as much from the added promotion of the "holiday" as it does to promote it with its popular in-store fundraiser.

- Lastly, Macy's *Believe* campaign has kids dropping off letters to Santa at local Macy's stores in the weeks before Christmas. Macy's donates $1 to Make-A-Wish, up to $1 million, to help grant wishes for children who have life-threatening diseases.

Recoup Is Revitalizing Cause Shopping

Entrepreneur Luca Pivato has a simple mission. Amid all the online shopping sites, he's convinced the world needs at least one cause shopping site where consumers can buy the things they want, at great savings, while they support the causes they love with each and every purchase.

(continued)

(*continued*)

That's why Pivato started Recoup.com.

With Recoup, businesses and nonprofits get their very own shopping pages. When customers buy an item, 10 percent of the sale goes to a Recoup charity partner of their choice. They also have the option at checkout to donate a portion or all their savings to the nonprofit.

The upside of Recoup to nonprofits is significant.

- **Recoup builds the nonprofit a customized shop and profile.** Nonprofits don't have the expertise or experience to build their own shopping site. With Recoup, they don't have to. Everything is done for them so they can focus on promoting the shop to their supporters and raising money.

- **Recoup populates the nonprofit's shop with offers from its business partners.** This saves nonprofits from the hassle of finding their own business partners and inking their own deals.

- **Recoup opens the nonprofit and its shop to a broader audience.** Although Recoup encourages the nonprofit to promote its shop to supporters, Pivato says most sales come from his company's promotion efforts, not the nonprofit's.

"Nonprofits are amazing organizations that do wonderful work in the world," said Pivato. "But they're not skilled marketers, and they need our help to raise money from businesses in the most efficient and effective way possible. Recoup helps them do that."

Nonprofits like Recoup because they can focus their energies on changing the world with the support of businesses, instead of building a shopping site and cold calling for partners.

"We got our first check from Recoup for $758.00," wrote Goodwill of Greater Washington D.C. "Not pocket change as
(*continued*)

far as we're concerned when it comes to online fundraising. We're very grateful to Recoup and the businesses and shoppers who choose to support us."

Businesses like Recoup because it's a turnkey cause solution that makes it easy for them to give back and reap the rewards of the cause-conscious consumer. Recoup will even match up the business with a cause that fits its target demographic. Recoup's commitment to sales is as strong as its social mission to make the world a better place. No margin, no mission.

The consumer is the big winner.

First, they get to spend their time on a *gorgeous* website that features stunning images that are as colorful and inspiring as the causes Recoup supports.

Second, consumers know exactly how much of each sale benefits the nonprofit. Recoup is perfect for consumers that are tired of buying products that say *A percentage of the proceeds from sales will benefit local causes*. How much of a percentage? From one sale or from the total sale? Which local causes?

Each item on Recoup clearly states which charity it supports and how much it will receive. You can learn more about the nonprofit on a profile page. If you'd rather choose another nonprofit to benefit from your purchase, you can do it right on the spot. Happy to donate more? You can do that at checkout and earn yourself a tax deduction.

Right now, Recoup is working with local causes in four markets: Washington, D.C., New York City, Baltimore, and Miami. If your nonprofit is in one of these cities, Recoup would love to hear from you.

"The key is that nonprofits recognize the value and opportunity that an online cause shopping site such as Recoup offers," Pivato explained. "Nonprofits, businesses, and consumers can do great things together. Recoup is where e-commerce becomes shopping for a cause."

STEAL THESE IDEAS!

1. You can combine an in-store fundraiser with another fundraiser from this book. For example, arts and crafts retail chain A. C. Moore asked customers at checkout to donate $1 to Easter Seals' *Act for Autism* campaign. To support the fundraiser, stores held a *Make and Take* craft event for children that taught them about autism. Although the event wasn't a fundraiser, A. C. Moore could have offered to donate an additional dollar for every craft project completed.

2. You can also use an in-store event to encourage a donation. Old Navy partnered with the National Center for Missing & Exploited Children to hand out free kid safety kits that included tips, an activity book, and a child ID. Safety kits in hand, customers were asked to donate $5 to the center in exchange for a coupon that gave 10 percent off their next Old Navy purchase.

FOR MORE INFORMATION

 You can see more examples of in-store fundraisers by visiting http://fwb40.us/188vnP1 or scan the QR code to view them on your smartphone or tablet.

CHAPTER THIRTY-TWO

Halopreneurs

In the aftermath of the Boston Marathon bombings in April 2013, there was a rush to produce products to raise money for victims of the attacks. There were mugs, shoelaces, bags, bandanas, and especially t-shirts.

I was surprised by how many products were being mass-produced by individuals instead of companies.

Do-gooders were flocking to *make-on-demand* sites like *Zazzle*, *CafePress*, and *Ink to the People* to custom design products to help the victims and to show their support for Boston.

These *on-demand* sites do more than just let people upload a t-shirt design. They handle order management, fulfillment, payment processing, and customer service. They allow cause-conscious individuals to operate as a business, and when a cause is involved, it is a business for good.

I call them *halopreneurs*.

To be clear, *halopreneurs* are different from *causepreneurs*, at least in my mind. [You can read more about causepreneurs in the feature for this chapter]. The latter are people that start and run cause businesses (TOM's Shoes is the most famous example). Halopreneurs are small-time operators that leverage a business platform—usually temporarily—to raise money for good causes.

Thanks to the flexibility of modern manufacturing and the convenience of technology, Halopreneurs are do-gooders with business resources at their fingertips.

COLLEGE STUDENTS' T-SHIRT RAISES $900K FOR BOMBING VICTIMS

Nick Reynolds and Chris Dobens just wanted to help. Like many Bostonians, Emerson College students Nick and Chris were glued to their television sets after two bombs exploded at the Boston Marathon finish line on April 15, 2013. Three people died and hundreds were injured.

"I looked at Nick and said why don't we come up with a t-shirt?" Chris recalled in an interview with Boston's CBS affiliate WBZ-TV.

Using *Ink to the People*, a make-on-demand site, the two picked a blue shirt with yellow letters that said *Boston Strong*. Their goal was to sell 110 shirts. Each shirt sold for $20 with $15 going to the victims after $5 in production costs was covered. They promoted the shirts all over campus, but it was social media—especially Facebook—that propelled the fundraiser.

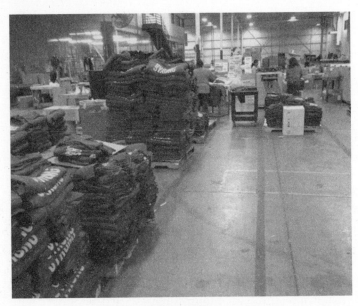

FIGURE 32.1

Boston Strong T-Shirts Are Ready to Ship from the Production Department at Ink to the People in Milwaukee, Wisconsin

Source: Courtesy of Ink to the People.

Nick and Chris didn't realize what they had started.

First, they coined the phrase *Boston Strong*, which became the battle cry for an angry city and a united nation. Second, when their campaign concluded two months later, they had sold 59,000 t-shirts! See Figure 32.1.

A fundraiser created on a whim raised more than $900,000 for the victims of the attack.

It's a feat that couldn't have been accomplished without the commitment of two do-gooders, social media savvy, and a company equipped to meet the challenge of making, printing, and distributing nearly 60,000 t-shirts.

Today, Nick and Chris have settled back into college life. But their time as *halopreneurs* has sparked new ideas, like publishing a *Boston Strong* book with photos, stories, and quotes.

Maybe Nick and Chris will use a publish-on-demand site like Lulu.com to make and sell books, just as they used Ink to the People for t-shirts!

HOW IT WORKS IN 1-2-3

1. The halopreneur identifies a make-on-demand site for the product they want to sell to benefit a nonprofit.
2. The price set for the product includes both the cost for producing it and a donation to the charity.
3. The halopreneur promotes the offering to their network and on social media sites.

THINGS TO REMEMBER

- Nick and Chris' *Boston Strong* t-shirt struck a chord with people who were stunned by the attacks and concerned for the victims. Although your product probably won't share the same urgency as Nick and Chris' did, you have to lead with emotion and give supporters a product they want to wear *and* share.
- Social-media skills are critical to your halopreneur's success. Good intentions are not enough. A social-media presence and community to market the product to will largely determine its

success. On demand sites offer online "shops" where you can sell your item(s). But don't count on them to drive traffic to your site. That's up to you!

- Nick and Chris didn't need to be asked to create a t-shirt to support the victims of the bombings. As is the case after many tragedies, they were inspired to act. These two halopreneurs were born, not made. But most nonprofits will have to rely on the latter. They'll have to identify potential halopreneurs and give them a nudge. Here's what they should be looking for.

  ○ Do they have marketing savvy? Do they understand and know how to use traditional and new media and how to build "buzz?"

  ○ Do they have an existing community to tap? Are they a graphic designer, entrepreneur, inventor, or artist that's created and sold other products?

  ○ Are they a member of the creative class? Yep, you want the hip and cool. These people are young and eager to express themselves. They're comfortable with technology, social media and make-on-demand sites.

KIND Lessons for Causepreneurs

I get calls every week from people that want to start a cause business. Good, intelligent, well-intentioned people who really want to change the world. They call. We talk. I never hear from them again.

They disappear because their business goes nowhere or fails. Here's why: They put the cause before the business, and violate the number-one rule of running one; *the best way to help a cause is to be a great business, first.*

I've been saying this for years. But no one listens! Here's someone you can listen to because he's the causepreneur you want to be.

(*continued*)

Ad Age interviewed Dan Lubetzky, the founder of KIND Healthy Snacks. In 2012 his company had sales of $125 million, double the revenues of 2011. Dan's business is cause driven, but he's not banking on cause to drive his business. Neither should you.

Looking to start a cause business? Follow Dan's rules.

Start with an Outstanding Product

Anything less won't do. U2's Bono and his wife, Ali Hewson, found this out the hard way a few years back with their clothing line Edun. When the clothes didn't meet consumer expectations, sales fell through the floor. "We focused too much on the mission in the beginning," explained Hewson to the *Wall Street Journal*." It's the clothes, it's the product. It's a fashion company. That needs to be first and foremost."

Like any good business, KIND leads with its products. The bar's value proposition says it all: *Kind to your body, your taste buds and the world*. It's not a coincidence that "the world" comes last. A bar that is tasty comes first.

Make Cause Just One Part of the Marketing Mix

KIND has grown through product quality, guerrilla marketing, social media, and targeting small stores—among other things. And its cause focus helps it stand out. Period.

But too many causepreneurs lead with the cause and think the waters will part at the mention of their social mission. Maybe its because *cause* begins with the letter *c*. But the only place *cause* comes before *product, marketing, social media, community*, and *distribution* is in the dictionary.

Expect About a 5 Percent Bump

That's how much cause will contribute to your success. It might be a little more. But most of the people I talk to are expecting a lot from dipping their product or service in the magical waters of cause. Lubetzky learned the hard way with a previous venture that you can't lead with cause. Almost everything needs to come before it. But, when added, cause makes everything better.

(*continued*)

(continued)

People ask me all the time if working with a cause will help their business. "If you're doing the other hundred things you should be doing to run a successful business, I would say yes," I tell them.

Where, when, why, and how to inject cause into a business is a mystery. I'm not sure when the timing is right, or how much is needed to goose sales or to change the world. But the first ingredient of a business isn't cause. Of that, I'm sure.

STEAL THESE IDEAS!

1. Although many people visit make-on-demand sites to create and sell t-shirts, there are other options.

   a. *Lulu.com:* On demand book publishing.

   b. *CreateSpace.com:* On demand books, CDs, and DVDs.

   c. *TasteBook.com:* On demand cookbooks.

   d. *TheGameCrafter.com:* On demand board and card games.

   e. *Spoonflower.com:* On demand fabric, wallpaper, decals, and gift wrap.

   f. *Ponoko.com:* On demand toys, housewares, furniture, jewelry and electronics.

2. Donor-advised funds (DAF) are another way individuals can leverage business services—in this case charitable giving accounts with sponsoring organizations—to support good causes. DAFs give individual donors the tools and resources they need to operate as their own family foundation. Among other things, donors can easily make donations of appreciated stock and assets, which without a DAF is kind of a hassle. Nonprofits should encourage donors to create DAFs and flag

and cultivate donors that already have one. Like make-on-demand sites, DAFs give people a good reason to give.

FOR MORE INFORMATION

 You can see more examples of halopreneur fundraisers by visiting http://fwb40.us/1ecY3cY or scan the QR code to view them on your smartphone or tablet.

CHAPTER THIRTY-THREE

Signature Cause Product Fundraiser

I recently visited Hershey, Pennsylvania, the home of Hershey's, the largest chocolate manufacturer in North America. Everywhere I turned there was something chocolate. I ate at the Chocolate Grill and when I checked into my hotel, The Hershey Lodge, they gave me a full-size Hershey's chocolate bar with my room key.

"I could get used to this place!" I said to the front desk clerk.

The hotel had a large store with all sorts of Hershey signature products. Of course, they sold Hershey chocolates of every variety, but they also sold beach towels, pillows, t-shirts, and slippers, all chocolate-themed and affixed with the Hershey logo.

I thought to myself, "How great is it to be a company that makes a product so admired that people will pay for the pleasure of owning something with your name on it."

But there's something even better: when a company sells that signature product and the proceeds go to a good cause.

WHITE CASTLE LIGHTS UP DONATIONS WITH SCENTED CANDLE

People love White Castle's hamburgers. They can't get enough of their signature meat and onion hamburgers served on a square bun.

White Castle gets so many letters from fans of their burgers that in 2001 they established the Cravers' Hall of Fame. Every year the chain chooses 5 to 10 letters to enter into the Hall of Fame.

As an experiment, White Castle introduced a meat and onion-scented candle that looks like the cardboard burger sleeve they pack the burgers in. Fans loved it and the initial order of 10,000 candles sold out in 48 hours. Best of all, proceeds from the candle benefited Autism Speaks, which has received over $100,000 since 2010.

The idea for the candle came from an Autism Speaks board member, Laura Slatkin, who is the CEO of Nest Fragrances. Laura is known to be the queen of home fragrances.

In an interview with ClutterMagazine.com Slatkin explained how the candle came to be.

"When I met Bill and Marci Ingram, two of the owners of White Castle, we laughed about producing a candle that smells like a Slider [what customers call a White Castle hamburger]," said Slatkin. "But, the more we talked about it, the more I thought to myself, 'What could be better than a candle that smells like a White Castle slider? It's what we all crave, most of all me!'"

HOW IT WORKS IN 1-2-3

1. Working with your business partner, identify a signature cause product to support your cause. As always, determine how much will benefit your cause, the minimum donation, and the start and end date of the program.

2. Develop the offering, the packaging, and the marketing that will support the campaign. The nonprofit and the business promote the fundraiser to their supporters and customers.

3. When can you expect to receive donations from the business? Monthly? Quarterly? Or at the end of the program?

THINGS TO REMEMBER

- Kitschy is the best word to distinguish a signature cause product from a traditional cause product (Chapter 13). The product is iconic, and created primarily for fans of the brand. For example, Firehouse Subs is well known for its pickles and the five-gallon buckets they come in. Fans of the chain love these buckets and use the old ones for gardening, painting, storage, and so forth. Firehouse sells the buckets for $2 each with all proceeds benefiting Firehouse Subs Public Safety Foundation.

How White Castle's Candle Can Teach You Not to Get Burned

About the same time White Castle was introducing its scented candle for Autism Speaks, Kentucky Fried Chicken was being crucified in the media for *Buckets for the Cure*. This fundraiser for Komen for the Cure involved pink buckets of fried chicken, of which 50 cents supported the breast cancer charity.

People were outraged that a health cause such as Komen had partnered with a fast food giant that was best known for buckets of calories, salt, and fat. Adding insult to injury, the same week that KFC launched *Buckets*, it released a new, heart-stopping menu item. *The Double Down* had bacon and cheese between two fried chicken breasts. KFC claimed to care about its customers' health. *The Double Down* showed the truth.

Although KFC and Komen battled detractors, no one complained about White Castle's candle. On Twitter, my followers questioned why White Castle had gotten a pass. "Why hasn't this caused the same uproar as KFC/Komen did?" one follower asked.

White Castle didn't spark the public's ire for a few good reasons.

White Castle's candle isn't trying to cure an ill it might have caused. Unlike KFC and their *Buckets*, White Castle isn't trying to help people with autism by selling a product that just might contribute to their condition in the first place. True or not, the American public doesn't believe a scented candle causes autism. They're not so sure about the link between fried chicken and cancer.

(continued)

(*continued*)

White Castle's candle is for loyalists. You'd have to be a big fan of White Castle's burgers to buy a candle that smells like one. The candle is made for burger fanatics. White Castle is simply giving their most loyal customers a chance to support a good cause. Conversely, KFC's *Buckets* included a major television and online advertising campaign to bring new, "pink" supporters into the hen house.

White Castle kept its distance. It doesn't connect its food with a health cause as KFC does. Perhaps White Castle took a page from McDonald's playbook. As a kid I remember McDonald's raising money for charities like the Muscular Dystrophy Association. But later it wisely stepped back from directly supporting health causes and focused instead on its own charity, The Ronald McDonald House, which offers families a place to stay when a child is receiving medical treatment.

The lesson for nonprofits is that you need to think twice about partnering with companies, such as fast food chains, which are lightening rods for controversy. As Komen learned with KFC, these partnerships can be a bird of a different feather.

STEAL THESE IDEAS!

1. A signature cause product can also capture the spirit of a well-known nonprofit. For example, companies such as Apple, Gap, and Starbucks have created signature red products to support Product Red and its fight against HIV in Africa. In this case, the cause is the star and the reason consumers buy it. Luckily, you don't have to be an internationally known charity founded by a rock star to get your own signature cause product. Produced and sold by Rhode Island based Alex & Ani, The Jimmy Fund, the fundraising arm of Boston's Dana Farber Cancer Institute, had a silver charm bangle for its 60th anniversary. The Jimmy Fund received 20 percent of

the $28 purchase price. That's how well known and loved The Jimmy Fund is in New England!

FOR MORE INFORMATION

 You can see more examples of signature cause product fundraisers by visiting http://fwb40.us/18MNA0N or scan the QR code to view them on your smartphone or tablet.

CHAPTER THIRTY-FOUR

Launch Fundraiser

Hundreds of thousands of businesses are started in the United States each year. And every one of them is eager to get off on the right foot.

Businesses have tried everything from music to celebrities to dancing to cupcakes to create a positive first impression. But consumers aren't buying it. They're shopping for something more substantial and filling than fancy hors d'oeuvres.

Opening a business or launching a product or service with a cause is a great way to make sure the customer's first impression is a *good one*.

ORANGE LEAF SWEETENS FIRST NYC STORE OPENING WITH CHARITY

Orange Leaf Frozen Yogurt is known for its self-serve, choose-your-own-toppings desserts. But when it came to opening their first store in Manhattan, "self-serving" was the last thing you could say about the company.

To celebrate its launch into the New York market in January, Orange Leaf partnered with Cookies for Kids' Cancer, a national nonprofit that sells cookies and uses bake sales to raise funds to support research for new and improved therapies for pediatric cancer. See Figure 34.1.

In addition to donating all proceeds generated during its grand opening to Cookies for Kids' Cancer, Orange Leaf's traditional toppings bar included a selection of cookies from the charity, available for New York customers to put on top of their frozen treats.

New product launches are another opportunity for a nonprofit tie-in.

FIGURE 34.1

Orange Leaf Store Opening Supports Cookies for Kids' Cancer

Source: Courtesy of Orange Leaf Frozen Yogurt.

To honor the hit NBC series *30 Rock*, Ben & Jerry's Ice Cream announced a new flavor, "Liz Lemon" after the show's star, who is portrayed by Tina Fey.

Proceeds from the sales of the new ice cream will benefit Jumpstart, an early childhood education nonprofit. Jumpstart's logo will appear on all of Ben & Jerry's "Liz Lemon" packaging, as well as on posters in Ben & Jerry's scoop shops and in other marketing materials.

Ben & Jerry's also hosted a *30 Rock* viewing party in New York City to watch and celebrate the series finale. A limited number of tickets were available, and all proceeds benefited Jumpstart.

HOW IT WORKS IN 1-2-3

1. Identify a business opening or product launch your nonprofit could be a part of.

2. Determine how your nonprofit will raise money with the launch or opening. Usually it's from a portion or percentage of the day's sales, but it can also be for a week or month.

3. Promote the launch or opening to your supporters.

THINGS TO REMEMBER

- Relax. A successful company, store or product launch won't hinge on your nonprofit. Your business partner knows that. Nevertheless, use your communication channels to encourage supporters to visit the business and try their products or services. Act like a true partner.

- The key is to know of new business and product launches before other local nonprofits. It helps to be a relentless networker and consumer of the latest news. Closely follow the pages of your local business journal and join your local Chamber of Commerce. I got some of my best leads on new-business openings from a board member who worked in commercial real estate. He knew which businesses were moving into Boston months before they actually opened.

Four Ways to Make PowerPoint Work for You, Not Vice Versa

I give a lot of presentations, and I listen to even more. They all share one thing: PowerPoint. If you've spent any time talking to businesses—either during your nonprofit career or in another position—I bet you've used or seen your share of PowerPoint.

(continued)

(*continued*)

I used to tell people to forget PowerPoint altogether—just talk to people! But I don't think that's realistic anymore. The expectation that speakers will use PowerPoint is so great that *you have to use it*. The challenge is how to use it well.

1. The Star is YOU!

Too often people lead with their PowerPoint presentations: pictures, videos, animation, crazy fonts, and templates. It's like a circus, and speakers see themselves more as a side act—clown car?—than the star of the show. Having an interesting PowerPoint is nice, but it doesn't compare to putting the time and work into an outstanding speech.

2. Use PowerPoint to do Something You *Can't Do*

PowerPoint should increase your listeners' understanding of whatever you're talking about. For example, you can talk all day explaining what a donation box is (Chapter 3), but wouldn't it be easier to just show one—and some of the different variations—on a PowerPoint slide for all to see?

3. Save Handouts until the End

Some people think it's a good idea to hand out your presentation in advance so listeners won't have to write everything down. The problem is that, unless you're Tony Robbins, they'll probably take more interest in your handout than they will in you. Why give them another reason *not* to listen to you? Instead, announce at the beginning of your speech that you'll hand out your presentation when you're finished. Encourage them to rest their pens and give you their full attention.

4. Manage the Things You Can't Control

Expect attendees to be on their smartphones and tablets throughout your presentation. They'll be texting, e-mailing, looking at cute baby pictures, and watching funny videos of puppies and kittens. It's an inescapable part of modern life and our mobile culture. Use it to your advantage.

(*continued*)

In this case, PowerPoint is your friend. For listeners updating their social networking sites, give them hashtags and pithy quotes to share with the world. I tell my listeners, "Tweet this." And with my thickest Boston accent I add, "You're friends will think you're wicked smahhht!" Add QR Codes on your slides that attendees can scan with their smartphones to see relevant content.

Remember, PowerPoint is a good servant but a poor master. Make it work for you and your audience.

STEAL THESE IDEAS!

1. Virtual grand openings or launches are another opportunity for fundraisers. For example, when New York based Retreat Boutique launched its online thrift store proceeds from sales on the site supported victims of domestic violence.

2. Use the launch fundraiser to launch another fundraising effort. For example, let customers know at a store opening that, in addition to donating a percentage of sales, the company is making an additional donation to your organization for every new "Like" of its Facebook page (see Chapter 16) through the end of the week. Or use the occasion to announce an upcoming shop-walk (see Chapter 21) in the downtown area to support your organization.

3. Pop-up stores are becoming a popular way for out-of-town businesses to get a toehold in the communities where they eventually want permanent businesses. New York's Luke's Lobster plans to open a location in Boston sometime soon. To generate interest, Luke's opened a pop-up shop in Boston for three days. All the proceeds supported the fund established to support the victims of the Boston Marathon bombings. Since companies that host pop-up stores are coming from outside

the area, your knowledge and contacts in the community may be helpful to them in setting up shop for a test run—you'll both benefit from the partnership.

FOR MORE INFORMATION

 You can see more examples of launch fundraisers by visiting http://fwb40.us/19HgjoY or scan the QR code to view them on your smartphone or tablet.

CHAPTER THIRTY-FIVE

Building Fundraiser

When a nonprofit works with a business, they can raise money from employees (e.g., Dollars for Doers, Chapter 36), customers (e.g. Register Programs, Chapter 2) and from the business itself (e.g., Percentage-of-Sales, Chapter 1). But what about from the physical building the company is located in?

No, I'm not suggesting you start probing office-building walls for hidden stashes of loot. But I am encouraging you to look at office buildings and other physical assets businesses have as opportunities to raise money.

CLIMBCORPS HELPS UNFIT TAKE STEP IN RIGHT DIRECTION

ClimbCorps is the brainchild of one of Boston's best hospitals, Brigham & Women's, and Steve Biondolillo, a leader in the walk fundraising movement in this country. In 1984, Steve coined the term *signature event*, which nonprofit professionals have used since to describe their major fundraising events.

Building fundraisers are not new. The American Lung Association's *Fight for Air Climb*, has been around for years. But in designing ClimbCorps, the Brigham and Steve had a bolder vision for America's stairwells.

In January 2013, ClimbCorps hosted the first set of climb-a-thons to raise awareness and funds to help fight heart disease, the leading cause of death in the United States. More than 1,000 people participated in *ClimbAmerica* and together they raised $75,000. See Figure 35.1.

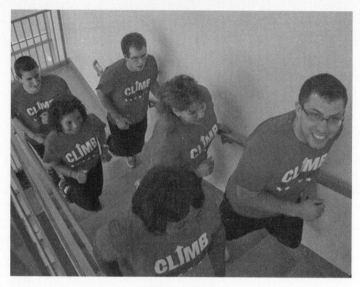

FIGURE 35.1

ClimbCorps Is Aiming to Turn Stairwells into Health Clubs

Source: Courtesy of Biondolillo Associates.

ClimbCorp is a service corp—similar to those run by City Year and AmeriCorps—but it's the first to focus on health and wellness. ClimbCorp service members organize Climb Clubs in some of Boston's tallest buildings. During lunchtime and after work, they lead stair-climbing programs for employees in 10 buildings.

When they're not leading climbing programs in buildings, ClimbCorps service members are busy in the community educating a variety of groups about heart health and how easy it is to get started with their own ClimbCorps program.

ClimbCorps will soon launch a National Climb Society in high schools nationwide to engage students in health and wellness and to organize a semester-long climb event that encourages students to be and stay active.

The climb society reflects the Brigham's aspirations to bring ClimbCorps to every stairwell in America. With heart disease, inactivity, and obesity being serious issues in every corner of this country, and plenty of empty stairwells in office buildings everywhere, ClimbCorps is a step in the right direction.

HOW IT WORKS IN 1-2-3

1. Working with your business partner, identify an appropriate fundraiser for the building. It can happen inside, outside, or on the grounds of the building.

2. Promote the fundraiser to employees within the building. If the building is an office building with other businesses, work with the building's management company to promote the event.

3. Safety is your number-one priority. Make sure you have any required permits, insurance, and are following building procedures.

THINGS TO REMEMBER

- Your success in working with companies hinges on looking inward to detect strengths and assets you never thought you or your business partner had. Does your nonprofit or business partner have a physical space that is unique and desirable? Do visitors respond with interest, curiosity, even awe when they see it? You might just have something to fundraise around.

- Invite people you trust and admire to share their insights about your physical space. Like advertising executive Peter Brown did in the Pine Street Inn story that follows, they may see an opportunity you don't.

- There are two target audiences for building fundraisers. First, you have the individual companies within the building. Second, you have the building managers or owners. Although most nonprofits smartly target the former, don't overlook the building managers and owners. Not only can they open doors to all the businesses in a building, but they may also open doors at other buildings they manage.

Homeless Shelter Raises Money from Tower of Power

Companies aren't the only organizations with physical assets for fundraisers. Nonprofits are sometimes housed in unique or old buildings that have their own fundraising potential.

In the case of a Boston homeless shelter, it took a business executive to see the fundraiser that was right over its head.

Driving the expressway into downtown Boston, advertising executive Peter Brown saw something the staff and donors at Boston's best-known homeless shelter had never seen: a tower with a pot of gold at the top.

Located in a nineteenth-century building, the Pine Street Inn has a tower that was modeled after the Palazzo Pubblico, the old town hall in Siena, Italy.

But when Brown looked up, he didn't see history, he saw dollar signs. Visible by commuters from several main Boston roadways, the tower was a perfect place for billboard advertising.

The rest is history. Brown convinced the shelter that they had a premium piece of advertising space. The Pine Street Inn eventually raised over $2 million, which they used to restore the tower to its former glory.

Unfortunately, the nonprofit bowed to public pressure after the tower was repaired and removed the ads. The timing couldn't have been worse. The economy soon sputtered and the extra cash would have certainly helped Pine Street.

The bigger lesson for nonprofits is clear. *We all have assets—* sometimes physical assets—from which we can raise money. But we don't always realize what those assets are. Sometimes we need people like Peter Brown who can point them out to us. Even then, we need to be open-minded enough to accept and act. It takes two people to hear the truth.

Assets come in all shapes and sizes. For the Pine Street Inn, it was their tower. What's your *tower of power?*

STEAL THESE IDEAS!

1. Don't stop with office buildings! Look at every physical space as an opportunity to raise money. Hotels have turned their pools into swimming fundraisers. Companies have converted empty office spaces into rent-free homes for nonprofits. Why stop inside the building? Companies have opened their roofs to community gardens and even allowed fundraisers to rappel down the side of their buildings. Supermarkets have turned their parking lots into party areas with games and food, with all proceeds going to charity. Cruise lines have encouraged guests to walk, run, shop, and party for causes while aboard. The opportunities are everywhere, but you have to find them. As Sherlock Holmes told Dr. Watson, it's not enough to see, you must *observe*.

2. If you live in or near a major city, research if there is an organization that connects nonprofits in office buildings. Here in my hometown of Boston we have a nonprofit called Building Impact that does just that. Working with the office building community, Building Impact helps organize everything from employee blood drives to building-wide fundraisers. Building Impact has expanded to Hartford, Connecticut, and could be in your city next. But a similar organization may already exist in your community.

FOR MORE INFORMATION

 You can see more examples of building fundraisers by visiting http://fwb40.us/14Lk9di or scan the QR code to view them on your smartphone or tablet.

CHAPTER THIRTY-SIX

Dollars for Doers

Nonprofits say they want to move beyond corporate handouts to corporate partnerships, but ignorance, not opportunity, may be what's holding them back. One example is the Dollar for Doers program (also known as Volunteer Grants) that many companies offer. See Figure 36.1 to see how these programs work.

Dollars for Doers is a matching gift program for volunteerism that rewards volunteer hours with a company donation to the nonprofit. The typical formula is $10 for each hour spent volunteering, although it's not uncommon to see corporate matches of $20 per hour or more.

The good news is that in 2011 the Committee Encouraging Corporate Philanthropy (CECP) reported that Dollars for Doers had been the most frequently offered employee-volunteer program.

The bad news is that employee participation in the program stinks. Only 7 out of 100 employees apply for this cash incentive.

Employee-giving experts have dubbed Dollars for Doers programs the incentive that nobody wants. Here's how to profit from what everyone else is missing.

HOW ONE NONPROFIT IS RAISING DOLLARS FROM DOERS

To learn more about Dollars for Doers I knew I had to speak to a nonprofit that worked with a lot of volunteers. If it was really true that only 7 out of 100 employees applied for this money, I needed an

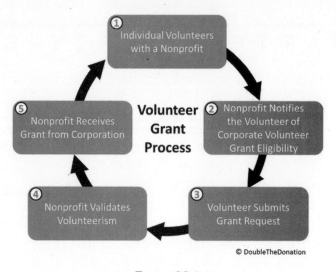

FIGURE **36.1**

The Dollars for Doers (aka Volunteer Grants) Process
Source: Courtesy of Double the Donation.

organization that had so many volunteers that they'd be sure to have experience with the program.

Boston-based Cradles to Crayons helps poor children from birth through age 12 with the essential items they need to thrive, at home, at school and at play. This includes everything from shoes to coats to backpacks and many other important items.

Cradles to Crayons collects these items from community organizations and companies. But they don't get collected, sorted, and distributed on their own. Cradles to Crayons relies on volunteers to help them—and not just a few. Last year, 20,000 volunteers worked in its "Giving Factory."

I knew I had found the right nonprofit!

My point person was Jennifer White, director of development and strategic partnerships, and she knew all about Dollars for Doers.

"We're very familiar with the program," she said. "We always ask our volunteers if they have a program and follow up with them afterward."

Jennifer conceded the biggest challenge is getting employees to log their hours with their company.

"If employees can log their hours online we get a better and faster response," she said. "But if they have to print out a form and get it to another department in the company . . . well, you know what happens."

"It's also not always easy to determine which companies offer Dollars for Doers," said Jennifer. "Companies don't seem to promote it as much as its sister program, matching gifts."

And unlike matching gifts, nonprofits working with Dollars for Doers programs have to jump more hurdles to get the money. Companies often require a certain number of volunteers or hours—or both—to trigger a donation.

For example, department store chain Kohl's requires that a group of five or more employees volunteer together for three consecutive hours before a grant is awarded. Some companies take it one step further and put eligible nonprofits into a pool from which grant recipients are chosen.

Nonprofits lose out when companies make it too challenging to receive a grant. But companies may be missing an opportunity as well.

"I'm surprised how few companies track employee volunteer hours," said Jennifer. "They just don't keep track of this—but we do. It's there for the asking."

In a time when consumers are as interested in a company's community footprint as they are in product and price, employee volunteerism may be the deal that shoppers can't resist.

HOW IT WORKS IN 1-2-3

1. After volunteering with a nonprofit, the employee volunteer completes their company's Dollars for Doers application and submits it to the nonprofit.

2. The nonprofit verifies the volunteer's activities and hours and forwards the form to the company for review.

3. If the request meets the program guidelines, a check is issued and sent to the nonprofit in the employee's name.

THINGS TO REMEMBER

- Take the lead in educating volunteers. Ask volunteers if they know about the Dollar-for-Doers program where they work. If they're not sure, help them find out. Most employees don't know their company has a program in place.

- Don't give volunteers an excuse to forget. Do everything you can to remind volunteers to submit their hours to employers so you can receive your *FREE* money.

Five Ways to Promote Your Dollars for Doers Program

1. Use tweets and Facebook updates to promote the program to social media users.

2. Write a blog post or article for your newsletter, profiling a volunteer that donated through his or her company's Dollars for Doers program.

3. Add a postscript to thank-you letters mentioning the program and asking volunteers to participate.

4. Online sites, such as Double the Donation (www .doublethedonation.com), help nonprofits solicit matching gifts and offer nonprofits free pre-made banner ads for their websites.

5. Add a line promoting the Dollars for Doers program to the e-mail signature of development officers that work in this area.

STEAL THESE IDEAS!

1. Focus on building your database of companies that have Dollars for Doers programs. Contact organizations that build memberships based on corporate volunteering and workplace giving. In the United States, contact the Association of Corporate Contributions Professionals (ACCP) or the Business for Social Responsibility. In Canada, contact the Canadian Business for Social Responsibility. Ask which of their members have a Dollar for Doers program and then poll your volunteers to see who works at those companies.

2. Treat your company as a partner, and ask them to return the favor. Encourage them to simplify the application process so employees can quickly complete their request. Ask them to design a smartphone app so employees can immediately log their hours after volunteering. Finally, suggest they designate a champion of the program within the company to ensure the program runs smoothly and is a source of company pride.

3. Use the program to start a friendly competition. If you have volunteers from different companies, challenge them to a contest to see who can volunteer the most and raise the most money with the Dollars for Doers program. Volunteers will have fun, you'll raise money, and companies that don't have Dollars for Doers programs will soon hear from employees that want to compete.

4. Partner with companies that offer the programs. If your organization works with volunteers, double your efforts to recruit them from organizations with Dollars for Doers programs.

5. Don't stop with current employees or with cash. Some companies offer Dollars for Doers support for retirees. Others, like Southwest Airlines, offer tickets instead of cash. With *Tickets for Time* employees can earn free airline tickets for their favorite charity when they document volunteer hours.

FOR MORE INFORMATION

 You can see more examples of Dollars for Doers programs by visiting http://fwb40.us/1fZzTOJ or scan the QR code to view them on your smartphone or tablet.

CHAPTER THIRTY-SEVEN

Special Occasion Fundraiser

A study released in 2012 showed that companies donate more around big events like the Superbowl or the Olympics.

This isn't groundbreaking news for those of us who work in corporate giving and sponsorship. But it definitely punctuates the value of massing your fundraisers around special occasions, holidays, and "big events."

For example, since the fall of 2012, I've tracked as many holiday fundraisers with businesses that I could find (e.g., Christmas, Halloween, Independence Day, Superbowl, World Aids Day, etc.) at Pinterest.com/joewaters.

The spike in fundraisers was dramatic, especially during the holiday season.

The lesson for nonprofits is that these special days and moments are your fundraising friends, and although you may find the marketplace crowded with other charities, businesses and consumers will be more responsive to your appeals on days when giving is second only to buying.

FIVE REASONS TO HAVE A HALLOWEEN FUNDRAISER

Halloween is my favorite holiday. You can ask my kids. I have more fun dressing up and decorating the house than they do.

But I'm no expert. That's why I talked to someone who is: Sal Perisano, CEO of Massachusetts based iParty Stores. iParty has 52 stores in New England and Florida. The chain was voted *Party Retailer of the Year* in 2008. Sal knows his stuff about candy corn, costumes, and fog machines!

Here are Sal's top five reasons for why Halloween is a treat, not a trick, for fundraising.

1. Halloween is Nipping at Santa's Heels

Nearly 70 percent of Americans celebrate Halloween. In 2012, they spent $6.8 *billion*, nearly double what they spent in 2005. This makes Halloween the second largest consumer holiday after Christmas.

And like Christmas, Halloween shopping is starting earlier than ever. I saw Halloween candy for sale in stores in July!

"Moms are buying costumes two months out," said Sal. "They're finding all sorts of uses for them, including kids' pajamas. Our first advertisements for Halloween run in August."

The popularity of Halloween with consumers makes the holiday a good bet for nonprofits.

2. Halloween is for Everyone

Children, teens, adults, even the family pets are getting in on the Halloween fun. Kids love it for the candy. Teens love the parties. Adults love the chance to let loose. And pets love it for—what else —the costumes.

"Our hottest selling costumes are for pets," said Sal. "We sell over 90 pet costumes online. People dress their pets up as sharks, Elvis, even a strip of bacon."

Halloween puts the fun in FUNdraising for everyone.

There'll be no lack of ideas or participants for Halloween fundraisers, which should bolster nonprofits' confidence of success.

3. Halloween is Big Business

Every type of business is trying to grab a piece of the multi-billion-dollar Halloween pie. A car wash near my house even offers haunted car washes for fans of the holiday, and every dollar they collect that day goes to a good cause.

The good news for nonprofits is that they don't have to "sell" businesses on Halloween sponsorships and fundraising. Businesses get it and understand the value of the holiday.

4. Halloween Social Media Activity is Scary

Expect lots of updates, tweets, pins, and posts this October. Sal predicts that Halloween will soon rival events like the Superbowl as celebrators use social networks to share party invitations, costumes, tricks, and pictures.

"People are photographing themselves in our stores with masks and costumes and uploading the pictures and videos to Instagram, Twitter, and YouTube," Sal said. "Halloween is ideal for social media contests and hashtag fundraisers."

5. Nonprofits are Cashing in on Halloween

Sal knows firsthand just how successful a Halloween Fundraiser can be. iParty hosted an annual October fundraiser that raised $160,000 for one of his favorite nonprofits.

Thanks to the current zombie craze, nonprofits are having success with fundraisers that cater to the undead, like zombie runs and walks.

Sal thinks Halloween can support nonprofits in a bunch of ways.

"Let's face it, Halloween is a great time to have a company-wide blood drive," he said. "The other opportunity is for product donations. Several homeless shelters in Boston accept candy donations from companies.

"For these people, getting candy is the treat it's supposed to be," he added. "The key is that you're asking companies to give when they have extra product and the inclination to give."

HOW IT WORKS IN 1-2-3

1. After you choose the special occasion around which your fundraiser will be held, work with your business partner to pick the right fundraiser.

2. If your nonprofit doesn't have a natural connection with the occasion (e.g., a food bank doing a fundraiser over Thanksgiving), be creative and link your cause in another way. See the "bauballs" example I use later. Remember, lead with emotion.

3. Depending on the type of fundraiser you're working on, learn from holiday marketers and start early! Some early momentum will make sure your fundraiser is in full swing around the special occasion. For example, we started Halloween fundraising as early as the middle of September. Two weeks before Halloween our business partners were tested and primed for the key push through the holiday.

THINGS TO REMEMBER

- A natural connection between your nonprofit and the special occasion isn't necessary, but it does help. This means food banks should focus on Thanksgiving. Children's charities can target Christmas, and women's groups can fundraise on Valentine's Day or in May around Mother's Day. Finally, nonprofits that support U.S. soldiers at home and abroad can adopt Memorial Day, Veterans Day, and Independence Day. Remember, the key is to tap the spirit of the occasion. Men's health issues are not top of mind during the holidays. But an enterprising business and male cancer charity came up with "bauballs," a scrotum-shaped Christmas ornament. They took the spirit of the season to a new level!

- Some occasions require more sensitivity than others. Since 2001, brands have struggled to hit the mark on Patriot Day, September 11. One brand tweeted a message of remembrance with a picture of its red and white potato chip bags arranged as an American flag. Social media users quickly cried foul and the brand removed the picture.

- Special occasions bring out the generosity out in people, but don't take without asking. Over the holidays, a restaurant in New York City thought it would be a good idea to raise money for a food bank by adding a dollar to every diner's tab—whether they agreed to it or not. Not everyone responded with holiday cheer.

Ambush Your Competition and Bring Home the Gold

In 2012, the Olympic Committee took unprecedented steps to protect its brand against rogue marketers that sought to align their companies with Olympic glory without paying the hefty sponsorship fee.

As the Olympic torch made its way around the world to London, it had bodyguards and two lawyers assigned to stop ambush marketing on behalf of unlicensed products. See Figure 37.1.

Fortunately, your nonprofit competitors aren't taking the same precautions. That means you should exploit their lapse and ambush their programs, events, and ideas. Good fundraisers borrow. Great fundraisers steal!

FIGURE 37.1

The Olympic Torch Had Plenty of Company, Including Two Lawyers
Source: Photo courtesy of Dean Thorpe via Flickr.

(*continued*)

(continued)

Target Their Partners

The best place to find your next corporate partner is in the arms of another. Companies partner with nonprofits for a variety of reasons, and the warm embrace may not be as mutual as you might think. If you can't break them up, you might be able to at least add yourself to the mix. Many companies support more than one nonprofit. You'll have more luck targeting a business that already supports a cause than one that is new to supporting one.

Keep Your Enemies Closer

If you can't beat your competitors, join them. Find a way that you can work with them that allows you to raise money. A few years ago, an investment firm I worked with wanted to host an event to support a cause, but they couldn't decide which of their three favorite charities should get the money. We made it easy for them. We held an event that combined the resources and assets of all three charities and we each got $50,000. A third of something is better than nothing.

Piggyback on Their Events

When I did marathon fundraisers for a Boston nonprofit, we ambushed the most famous road race in the world—the Boston Marathon—by selling sponsorships to businesses that wanted to be on the marathon course but didn't want to pay for an official sponsorship. As a charity, we were allowed to set up cheering sections along the course to aid our runners. Our corporate partners joined us and marketed their products and services to the large crowds lining the course.

Use your Halo

Being a charity allows you to get away with certain things. You can get stuff for free (or almost free) that others can't. You get reduced rates on permits, licenses, and fees because you're a 501(c)(3). A few years ago, Kentucky Fried Chicken ambushed the Superbowl when it offered a quarter of a million dollars to the player that flapped his arms like a chicken in the

(continued)

end zone. A self-serving promotion for KFC, for sure, but not so unacceptable considering the money didn't go to the player, but to his favorite cause.

Ambush marketing isn't for everyone. It takes guts and thick skin. You'll make a few enemies, but you might just bring home the gold.

STEAL THESE IDEAS!

1. There's another time after which company donations spike: after a natural disaster or a tragedy. This isn't the time to exploit misery for your nonprofit's gain, but if your nonprofit is assisting in the aftermath, or would respond to a similar tragedy in your community, this is your chance to raise money while your mission is top of mind. Just remember that you're also under a microscope, and should proceed with these three things in mind.

    First, show potential donors how their support of your organization will directly help the victims of the tragedy. You don't want people to think that you're just trying to exploit a bad situation to raise some money.

    Second, be clear on how much will be donated from your fundraiser. After the Boston Marathon bombing, I pinned nearly 100 products and services that benefited the victims. But the disclosure information on many of these items varied from nothing to ambiguous ("A portion of funds raised") to confusing ("A portion of net proceeds"). This served as fresh fodder for our hometown newspaper that ran a story titled "Transparency Lacking in Bombing Victims' Funds." This isn't the kind of press you want for your fundraiser.

    Finally, you and your business partner should publicize the results of your fundraiser. This isn't showboating. People want and need to know the results of your fundraiser, especially in the aftermath of a tragedy when awareness of your efforts is much higher.

2. During difficult economic times or after a tragedy or disaster, holiday parties and outings seem like an extravagance. Maybe your nonprofit could benefit from a company realigning its priorities or scaling back on employee gifts, parties, and client swag.

3. Special occasions don't have to be annual. They can be once in a lifetime! Nonprofits in the United Kingdom capitalized on the birth of the royal baby in 2013 with appeals, promotions, and fundraisers.

4. Some special occasions are less formal than Christmas or Thanksgiving. In 2013, car maker Volkswagen used the Discovery Channel's annual airing of *Shark Week* to launch a hashtag fundraiser to help save sharks. The auto maker donated $2 for every tweet with the hashtag #VWsharkweek.

5. Instead of special occasions, focus on *special moments*. A UK charity is asking parents and children to donate the money they get from the Tooth Fairy. These *Tooth Fairy Heroes* will help save elephants from being killed for their tusks!

FOR MORE INFORMATION

 You can see more examples of special occasion fundraisers by visiting http://fwb40.us/17YZrZR or scan the QR code to view them on your smartphone or tablet. Additionally, I have separate boards dedicated to Halloween, Christmas, Veterans Day, the Superbowl etc. You'll find them on my main Pinterest board, http://pinterest.com/joewaters.

CHAPTER THIRTY-EIGHT

Coupon Book Fundraiser

Coupon-book fundraisers are pinups (Chapter 15) with incentives. Like pinups, cashiers sell coupon books at checkout to raise money for good causes. But instead of appealing solely to the shopper's charitable side, the cashier offers an incentive to shoppers to give: money-saving coupons.

A typical cashier pitch for a coupon book would go like this: "Would you like to donate a dollar to feed hungry children? As a thank you, you'll receive these coupons that offer $50 in savings."

If you're like me and think that the recipe for most giving is a pound of self-interest and a teaspoon of idealism, coupon-book fundraisers make a lot of sense.

GROCERY-STORE CHAIN SUPPORTS EASTER SEALS WITH COUPON BOOKS

For the past 22 years, Food Lion has been supporting Easter Seals at hundreds of locations in the mid- and south-Atlantic states.

The inaugural program was a modest one in its North Carolina stores. It raised $20,000. Twenty-one years later, Food Lion has raised $33 million for Easter Seals.

For the past several years, Food Lion has been selling a coupon book. For a $1 donation, shoppers receive $9.50 in savings from Kraft and Procter & Gamble.

Food Lion supports the month-long coupon-book fundraiser with several percentage-of-sales programs that occur simultaneously. For every 24-pack of Food Lion water purchased during the campaign, Food Lion makes a 25-cent contribution to Easter

Seals, up to $250,000. Specially marked General Mills cereal-box purchases generate a 15-cent donation up to $50,000. Unilever, makers of Breyers Ice Cream, promotes its donation of $10,000 on specially marked cartons of vanilla ice.

HOW IT WORKS IN 1-2-3

1. Working with your business partner, design, print, and ship the coupon books.
2. At checkout, cashiers ask customers if they want to donate to charity.
3. The cashier collects the money and the customer gets the coupon book.

THINGS TO REMEMBER

- Is the coupon offering a good deal? Remember, your non-profit's reputation is on the line too. If consumers think the coupon stinks (e.g., lousy deal, lots of exclusions) they may extend that thinking to your organization.
- Work closely with your business partner to ensure the coupon is correct, and have them sign off on the final proof before it goes to the printer. Have them review the offer again when it comes back from the printer. The last thing you want is your business partner to be stuck with a bad deal that costs them a lot of money and hurts their reputation.
- After the offer, the most important thing on a coupon is an expiration date. Make sure each coupon in your book has one!
- Ask your business partner(s) to keep track of coupon redemptions. This is an excellent metric to renew a partnership and/or to recruit another partner. One business partner I worked with insisted on giving each of its coupons an individual serial number so they could track it from cashier to consumer to cashier again.

Three Reasons Your Register Fundraiser Should Have Coupons

I'm a big fan of using coupons at the register. They have an immediate value when cashiers are asking shoppers to support our cause.

"Would you like to donate a dollar to help sick kids? As a thank you, you'll receive $10 in savings."

It's a great one-two punch! But there are other good reasons to use coupons.

1. **Coupons are hot!** Because of the recession, coupon use has surged 35% since 2008, according to Inmar, a coupon clearinghouse. Consumers redeemed a whopping 3.5 billion coupons last year. Couponing has gotten so big that "couponers"—as they like to call themselves—now have their own show, the TLC reality series *Extreme Couponing*. A coupon book fundraiser gives consumers what they want.

2. **Coupons are overwhelmingly clipped, not downloaded.** The majority of coupons still come from print inserts— although online coupon offers are growing fast. If you still think handing out coupons is old school, think again. The National Newspaper Network released a report in 2011 that showed 91 percent of consumers aged 25 to 34 use newspaper coupons. These young consumers are also strong supporters of businesses that support good causes. Couponing and causes are a perfect match!

3. **Coupons can prove that a program is working.** Coupon redemptions during or after a coupon-book fundraiser is a metric for tracking the success of your program. A partner I worked with was surprised when a coupon-book fundraiser we executed had brought in 1,100 coupon-bearing customers from cross-partner stores that generated an additional $400,000 in revenue.

STEAL THESE IDEAS!

1. You have two options with your coupon book. You can limit the coupons to your business partner, or you can include coupons from other businesses. If you choose the latter, the participating businesses can either agree to sell the books in their business or pay to be included in the book. Either way, you win.

2. You don't have to do a coupon book. I've also experimented with a coupon pinup that was a just as effective and a bit cheaper.

3. Speaking of saving money, why not put the skills of a *super couponer* to work for your organization? These people know how to save money and get things for free! That's just what Building Blocks did with couponer Elba Peterson. To help the needy families that Building Blocks serves, Elba used her couponing skills to help the organization. "We ended up getting 20 sausages for free from Dollar Tree with coupons—some allergy medication for free," Peterson told CBS-13 in Sacramento. "We went and got 80 boxes of Hamburger Helper. That feeds 40 families."

FOR MORE INFORMATION

 You can see more examples of coupon book fundraisers by visiting http://fwb40.us/1e65Bxn or scan the QR code to view them on your smartphone or tablet.

CHAPTER THIRTY-NINE

Watch-to-Give Fundraiser

Many facts surrounding online content are debatable. One that isn't is people prefer video to text. According to Nielson Wire, a whopping 147 million Americans regularly watch video on the Internet.

And it's not just kids watching cat videos on YouTube. In a Forbes study, business people said they are watching more video than ever, and one in four prefer video to text for business information. Small businesses are getting in on the act with plans to produce more video content this year.

Indeed, some experts are predicting that video will soon surpass text as the single most important tactic for content marketers.

Video is hot. And with its explosive growth has come fundraisers for nonprofits that tap the immediacy and appeal of online video. See Figure 39.1.

RAM TRUCK SCORES FOR CHARITY WITH "FARMERS" SUPERBOWL AD

The power of watch-to-give fundraisers was on display the night of Superbowl XLVII when Ram Truck aired *So God Made a Farmer*. Narrated by the late Paul Harvey, the two-minute spot celebrated the American farmer.

Ram Truck offered to donate one dollar for each view of the YouTube video—up to $1 million—to National FFA Organization to fight hunger in communities across the country. The video got more than 18 million views.

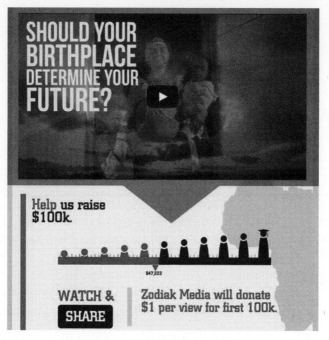

FIGURE 39.1

Zodiak Media Donated $1 per View up to $100,000 to Help Keep South African Children Out of Poverty

Source: Courtesy of Ubuntu Education Fund.

The intersection of advertising, online video, and cause proved to be a powerful one. Ram Truck's *Farmers* was a top pick among critics and viewers for best ad of Superbowl XLVII.

HOW IT WORKS IN 1-2-3

1. Working with your business partner, select a video to upload and decide on a donation per view. It's wise to set a maximum donation.
2. Pick a start and end date for the fundraiser.
3. At the end of the fundraiser, consult the statistics tab under the video for the total number of views, and other useful data.

THINGS TO REMEMBER

- A watch-to-give fundraiser can either promote a company or a nonprofit—or both.

- Promotion is key for a watch-to-give fundraiser. That's why many of these fundraisers involve companies with plenty of marketing muscle.

- You don't need a professionally produced video. You can record one on your smartphone. But don't pass up the chance to communicate a powerful message about your organization.

- More people than ever are watching videos on smartphones and tablets. Review your video to make sure it's as compelling on a 4-inch screen as it is on a desktop.

Making People Cry Isn't a Good Nonprofit Marketing Strategy

I talk a lot about the key role emotions play in fundraising. If you don't lead with emotion, you'll fail.

I also talk a lot about mobile technology, which will be a key driver of fundraising in the years ahead.

But here's the rub: Emotion and smartphones may not be a good mix.

That's my conclusion after reading about the research of A.K. Pradeep, founder and CEO of Nielsen NeuroFocus, on the connection between brainwave analysis and ad response.

Here's the bottom line:

As screen size decreases so does the viewer's emotional response to what they are watching.

Think about the implications for nonprofit marketing. You've worked hard to create a strong emotional message with your nonprofit videos but on smartphones it will leave

(*continued*)

(*continued*)

viewers with dry eyes. So, if you can't make people cry on their smartphones, what should your goals be?

Get Their Attention

Although you can't engage people emotionally on their phones, you can still get their attention. You might need to grab them with something totally unexpected, or emphasize another component such as audio. The background music to a video, among other things, may play a bigger role in getting and keeping a user's attention.

Timing is Everything

The impact of emotional messages depends on where and when it's viewed. This makes sense to me. When I had the chance to add a QR Code to a pinup sold at the register I didn't link it to a video on my nonprofit. Who has time to watch a video when you have to lug the groceries out to the car? Instead, I linked it to a question-and-answer page on the program so people could quickly find out who/what they just gave a buck to—a common question/complaint after shoppers donate at the register. But you might be more successful with a video if the QR Code is on a cause product that people can scan after they get home and have the time and inclination for a good cry.

Focus on Tablets

Nielsen's research shows that some of the emotion lost with smartphones is restored on their big brother, tablets. You may need two mobile strategies. One for tablets, the other for smartphones. The latter may require a more practical, utilitarian approach.

Of course, Nielsen's research isn't the final word on emotion and mobile technology. A lot depends on what emotion is being engaged.

Did I ever tell you the joke about the duck, the pig, and the farmer?

STEAL THESE IDEAS!

1. Apply to join YouTube's nonprofit partner program (www .youtube.com/nonprofits). Accepted partners receive many free benefits, including increased branding capabilities, the ability to receive donations through Google Checkout, and call-to-action overlays on videos.

2. Embrace the power of one. Your nonprofit's video should have one message, targeted at one audience, and it should conclude with one call to action. You've already earned a contribution because the viewer watched the video. Conclude your video with a clear to-do.

3. Need inspiration? Subscribe to The Daily DoGooder (www .thedailydogooder.com). It delivers one informative and compelling nonprofit cause video to your inbox daily. Annually, they produce the DoGooder Video Awards, which recognize the creative and effective use of video in promoting social good.

4. Don't stop with the eyes. Engage the other senses. Free music-streaming service Songza created a playlist for studying that raised money with each listen for Pencils of Promise, a nonprofit that builds schools in developing countries. The program raised enough to fund a new school.

5. Vine is a mobile app that allows users to create and post video clips. These video clips created with Vine have a maximum length of six seconds and can be shared or embedded on social networking sites such as Twitter. Earlier this year, Product RED broke the world record for most Vine videos ever created for a cause. To track the clips submitted, RED used the hashtag #REDworldrecord. Vine is just now gaining steam with users. There's no reason why your next watch-to-give fundraiser can't be on Vine.

6. An offshoot of watch-to-give is *upload-to-give*. This is when a company makes a donation for every video upload. For example, health information web site Healthline.com

WATCH-TO-GIVE FUNDRAISER

launched "You've Got This"—a video campaign that encouraged HIV patients to give hope and advice to the recently diagnosed. For every video created, Healthline donated $10 to the World AIDS Institute.

FOR MORE INFORMATION

 You can see more examples of watch-to-give fundraisers by visiting http://fwb40.us/16n86Xl or scan the QR code to view them on your smartphone or tablet.

■ **252** ■

CHAPTER FORTY

Business-to-Business Fundraiser

Most fundraisers in this book are meant for businesses that are "consumer facing," that is, the business sells directly to consumers (e.g., department stores, coffee shops, restaurants). They're called a B2C or business-to-consumer.

B2C fundraising dominates because it targets a large and lucrative audience: everyday consumers. After nearly two decades in fundraising, I'm convinced that there is more money and opportunity in a business's customers than there is in most company checkbooks.

That said, whenever I talk about B2C fundraisers, I'm invariably asked about fundraisers for businesses that sell to other businesses, not consumers.

If your potential partner is a manufacturer, law firm, construction company, commercial real estate firm or other type of B2B—business-to-business—this chapter is for you.

B2B FUNDRAISER DISPENSES FUNDS, HOPE TO HUNGRY KIDS

An innovator within its own industry of hygiene products, SCA Tork sought the same reputation in fundraising when it launched the company's first B2B fundraiser for Share Our Strength's *No Kid Hungry*.

The fundraiser involved SCA Tork's Xpressnap Dispensers, which is a snappy name for a napkin dispenser!

FIGURE 40.1

SCA Tork's Xpressnap Dispenses Support for *No Kid Hungry*
Source: Courtesy of SCA Tork.

For four months in 2012 the dispensers were discounted from $8 to $2 and $1 per dispenser was donated to *No Kid Hungry*. See Figure 40.1.

The company promoted the campaign through a trade press release targeting the food-service industry, an e-blast to its distributor network and direct sales conversations—all with information on *No Kid Hungry*.

The fundraiser surpassed SCA Tork's goal by $3,000. An added benefit was that it doubled the average monthly sales of Tork's napkin dispensers!

HOW IT WORKS IN 1-2-3

1. Working with your B2B partner, explore how they could support your organization (e.g., product line, employees, vendor relationships).

2. Choose a fundraiser that has clearly defined goals for both your nonprofit and B2B partner.

3. Promote the fundraiser through the appropriate channels. For example, SCA Tork didn't send a press release to its local newspaper. It reached out via email to its distributor network—a more appropriate and receptive network.

THINGS TO REMEMBER

- B2Bs sell stuff just like B2Cs do. They just sell it to businesses instead of consumers. When you look at it in these terms it's clear that many of the same fundraisers for B2Cs can be used for B2Bs. For example, there is a wonderful garden center near my house, but I can't buy my plants there. It's only open to approved gardeners and landscapers—credentials I don't have. But they have a cashier and register and can do a point-of-sale fundraiser. The challenge will be to adjust the promotion to fit these business customers.

- B2B partners want to benefit as much from their partnership as their B2C counterparts. Helping *No Kid Hungry* wasn't SCA Tork's only goal. According to Share Our Strength, the company sought to re-energize marketing tactics and sales for its signature line of Xpressnap Dispensers. B2B and B2C may be different, but they still want the same thing: win-win partnerships.

Ten Fundraising Ideas for B2B Companies

1. Percentage of Sales (Chapter 1)
SCA Tork sold its napkin dispenser for $1 and donated $1 to *No Kid Hungry*.

2. March Madness Fundraiser (Chapter 14)
Organize an office pool for the NCAA tournament, the Superbowl, or the Oscars! Encourage the company to involve its vendors and clients.

3. Dress-Down/Up Day (Chapter 24)
B2B companies can dress down on Fridays or dress up to support the hometown sports team.

4. Matching Gifts (Chapter 29)
B2B companies offer some of the most generous matching-gift programs in the business world. For example, Microsoft matches up to $12,000 annually per employee.

(continued)

(*continued*)

5. Dollars for Doers (Chapter 36)

D4D, also known as volunteer grants, are popular at B2Bs, including KPMG, Boeing and Eli Lily.

6. Payroll Deduction (Chapter 18)

If your B2B partner doesn't have a payroll deduction program, help them create one and include you in it.

7. Building Fundraiser (Chapter 35)

Where is your business partner located? Are they in a building that would be good for a fundraiser? Are they the anchor tenant in the tallest building in your city? Maybe they could help organize a stair-climbing fundraiser.

8. Donate Profits Day (Chapter 27)

Donate profits days aren't just for B2Cs. BTIG LLC, a global financial services firm, annually hosts Commissions for Charity Day. Over the past decade, these donate-profits days have raised over $24 million for children's charities.

9. Cash Donations (Chapter 9)

Some of the most successful companies in the world are B2B companies. They have cash gifts waiting for you!

10. Collection Drive (Chapter 22)

Ask employees to donate coats, food, school supplies, or whatever else your nonprofit needs. Again, have them reach out to their customers and vendors to support the effort.

STEAL THESE IDEAS!

1. You need a strategy for your B2B partners. For me, this meant reviewing my nonprofit's programs and events for opportunities that were *most applicable* to my B2B prospects and partners. For instance, the Boston nonprofit I worked for

was fortunate to receive charity waivers for the world's premiere road race, the Boston Marathon. They're called waivers because Boston is a qualifying race. This means you have to run a certain time in another marathon to earn a spot at the starting line in Hopkinton, Massachusetts, where the marathon begins. It's tough! That's why the BAA, the nonprofit arm that runs the marathon, gives waivers to select charities. Charity runners don't have to run a qualifying time, but they do need to raise money for the nonprofit that gave them the waiver. I used to say that getting marathon waivers was like printing money! You're guaranteed at least $4,000, but participants often raise more. These charity waivers were so popular I had a line out of the door of people to sign up and hand over $4,000. But knowing that I had plenty of fund-raising ideas for my B2C partners, I would specifically target B2B partners for whom I often had fewer options. Why encourage a department store chain to participate in my nonprofit's marathon program when they could easily do pinups or a percentage-of-sales program? Why not share the waivers with a construction company that was eager to support my nonprofit but hadn't found the right way to help. You need to look at each of your partners—B2C and B2B—and match them to the right fundraiser.

FOR MORE INFORMATION

 You can see more examples of business-to-business fundraisers by visiting http://fwb40.us/1d8uUMd or scan the QR code to view them on your smartphone or tablet.

CHAPTER FORTY-ONE

Fundraising with Businesses: Seven Steps to Success

I'm a blogger, author, consultant, speaker, and cause marketer. But I'm a fundraiser first. The reason is simple. I've spent nearly 20 years raising money for nonprofits. I know fundraising better than anything else. And I know how hard it is.

Like you, I've read a bunch of books and blogs on fundraising, sat in plenty of classes and courses, and listened to webinars and podcasts to glean some insights on how to better raise money with businesses.

I often finished a book or course enthused by what I had read or heard, but I was still a bit unsure, a tad unclear. I wanted to be crystal clear! I vowed that I would not leave my students stuck in the same gray area.

A lot of the information in this chapter is scattered throughout the book, but in this final chapter I want to highlight seven things every nonprofit must do to successfully raise money from businesses.

START BY LOOKING WITHIN

Your first step after reading this book should be an asset analysis of your organization. Look within your organization for existing company partnerships, or for things that would be of value to a potential business partner. These things may include:

- A successful fundraiser (e.g., walk, run, gala, etc.).
- A large donor base.
- A large, engaged following on social-media sites.
- A targeted demographic of supporters that are women, Millennials, moms, parents, men, pet owners, and so forth.
- A large employee base.
- A visible, busy, or sought after building or location.
- A strong, well-recognized brand that people know and respect.
- Vendors that value their relationship with you.
- A strong, emotional mission. Do you serve kids? Do you save puppies from the pound? Do you help wounded soldiers returning from Afghanistan?

One of the most valuable assets you can have is an existing connection to a company. I like to say that a company in hand is worth two waiting in the bush!

Maybe you have a CEO that personally supports your cause, but has yet to commit his or her company to your cause. Or perhaps your organization has a long-standing vendor relationship with a company that would be open to a fundraiser.

Nonprofits don't usually know where to start when it comes to raising money with businesses. That's because they have their sights set too high and miss the low-hanging fruit!

HAVE A TARGET, AIM FOR A BULL'S-EYE

Nonprofits often ask me what kind of company they should pick. "Oh, that's easy," I say. "The company that will say yes!"

Some people think I'm being a smart aleck, but I'm not. Finding a business is a tough job, so why not start with the easy ones first?

If you already have a company partner, you should count yourself lucky. Everything is easier and possible when you have a partner. Sadly, few nonprofits have one when they call me. They have plenty of creative fundraising ideas, but when I ask about a partner to help execute their plans, they have nothing.

So, if you're not fortunate to already have a company partner, how do you find one for your cause-marketing program?

To begin, think of your prospecting efforts as a target with a bull's-eye and two outer circles.

The Bull's-Eye—Supporters

The bull's-eye is your sweet spot and where you should aim. The companies within the bull's-eye are existing *supporters* of your organization.

These companies already give you money in some way. The CEO may be a major donor, or the company might be a sponsor or underwriter of a program or event. Either way, this company is a friend, supporter, and ally with whom you can kick off a partnership.

Companies that are supporters are already on your side and willing to experimenting and taking risks because they know and *trust you*. This is important, especially if this is your first program. First tries are rarely perfect, and these partners will have the patience and forgiveness you'll need to try, and try again.

The Inner Circle—Contacts

The first outer circle after the bull's-eye is populated with what I call contacts. You know these people and they know you. But they're not the supporters that the companies within the bull's-eye are because they haven't given you any money. However, they are familiar with your organization and are excellent secondary prospects.

Examples of good contacts are your organization's vendors. If you work at a large nonprofit you probably spend a lot of money with several vendors that can either join you in a cause-marketing program or introduce you to a company that can.

Another example of contacts is your board members' contacts. I once landed a meeting with a major convenience store chain because when I mentioned the owner's name to a board member she exclaimed, "I live next door to him!"

It's best to work from the inside out. Begin with companies within the bull's-eye, execute a program or two, and then shop your success and experience to the next circle of prospects that will need more convincing than your generous supporters did.

The Outer Circle—Suspects

The companies in the outer circle aren't even prospects. I call them suspects—that's how weak their connection is to you.

These companies have no connection with your organization. They may not have heard of you or you of them. This is the hardest circle to work, but it also has the most potential because, let's face it, there are only so many companies we can call supporters and contacts. If selling were as easy as pitching supporters and contacts, we wouldn't need sales people and fundraisers!

Remember, just as the second circle is harder to work than the bull's-eye, the outer circle is the most difficult one of all. Work the bull's-eye and inner circle first, because you'll gain valuable experience and references. You'll need these when you work the companies in the outer circle.

You might be thinking that you can just start at the outer circle and make cold calls. Not only is this not very fun, but it's not very effective either. It sometimes works—like finding a needle in a haystack—but when you're stuck at the outer ring where it's cold and lonely, a better option is to revisit the basics (e.g., cultivating individual donors, adding influential members to your board, building your brand, etc.) so one day you can score a fundraising bull's-eye.

GET THE BLESSING OF YOUR BOSS

Many of the strategies in this book will be new to you. They'll be new to your boss, too, and she may not share your excitement. But, you need her support, or you may not get the resources you need to be successful.

Your boss needs to be your ally, not your adversary or a passive observer. Here's how to keep your boss close when it may seem like you're worlds apart.

Persuasion is incremental. Do you really expect your boss to accept these new ideas overnight? People don't generally change their minds quickly or easily, so you need to be realistic about what you can accomplish and how long it will take. Setting goals that can move your agenda forward will keep you and your boss engaged, in sync, and motivated.

Share the glory. Just as you have a boss, your boss has one, too. So when your fundraising program is a big success, don't forget to share the credit with her. Fundraising with businesses requires a team effort. And every team member should be acknowledged and credited for his or her work, including your boss.

Share the burden. When a former boss of mine launched our business fundraising program he had to leverage some of his own credibility with senior management to begin an effort many were uncomfortable with. He knew he needed to involve others to sustain the momentum during those uncertain times. So he created a business-giving committee.

He packed it with knowledgeable, well-respected supporters and donors that established fundraising with businesses as an institutional priority. This was no longer one man's personal aspiration. It was the shared goal of some of the most well-respected supporters of the organization.

FOCUS ON BUILDING YOUR BRAND

Fundraisers ask me all the time how they can raise more money from businesses. I tell them the answer is simple.

They lean in.

"The key is actually three things," I whisper.

They reach for a notepad and pen.

"The key," I say, "is BRAND . . . BRAND . . . BRAND."

Although they initially shrug me off, they come around when I explain it to them.

Powerful nonprofit brands are like magnets. Things are attracted to them. Take national causes like Feeding America, Product RED, St. Jude Children's Research Hospital, and Children's Miracle Network. They do great work, and companies flock to partner with them.

In my hometown of Boston I don't have to look any further than The Jimmy Fund and Boston's Children's Hospital. Both attract companies that want to support their mission and bask in the aura of their well-deserved and well-known goodness.

Unfortunately, and probably like you, I've witnessed this from afar because none of the nonprofits I've ever worked for had particularly strong brands. My friend Mark Horvath of Invisible People, a Los Angeles nonprofit that serves the homeless, says "anonymity is death." It's why people don't help the homeless, and why people aren't rushing to support your nonprofit.

A brand is what people experience—what they feel—when they come into contact with a person, place, or thing.

Not long ago, my wife asked me if I could cut back on my beloved Starbucks coffee so we could send our kids to a good private college one day. She even offered to invest in a nice espresso machine.

"I think I would miss going into my favorite Starbucks more than I would miss the coffee," I told her. I just like the *feeling* I get going into a Starbucks. I love the smells, the conversation, the different products, the atmosphere, and so on. Starbucks' brand has a strong magnetic pull on me.

In short, it looks like the kids are going to public schools.

Good brands, whether for-profit or nonprofit, are as strong and addictive as anything Starbucks serves.

But as a nonprofit, how do you create that powerful brand? Jeff Brooks, a well-known nonprofit strategist, has a suggestion.

He says that a nonprofit brand is different from a for-profit brand. Instead of a look-at-me brand, it's a look-at-you brand. It recognizes that donors give to make good things happen, not to support a name on a building.

Instead of promising to be the coolest charity on the block, good nonprofit brands promise a fulfilling, information-rich experience that will maximize the donor's impact. It says two things:

1. Support us and you'll have a big impact.
2. We promise to show that impact clearly and dramatically.

I like Jeff's thinking because he's talking about creating and communicating a powerful experience, *a powerful feeling for the donor*.

Do you want to raise more money from everyone, including businesses? Take Jeff's advice and focus on building your brand. I don't know one nonprofit that's been wildly successful without one.

DON'T GIVE BUSINESS GIVING TOO MUCH ATTENTION

I estimate that a successful business-giving program can raise an additional 5 to 15 percent in additional revenue for your nonprofit. So, if you are a $3 million nonprofit, you'll raise approximately $300,000 from an established program.

You might raise a little more, maybe less, but if you're expecting to double your revenues with the strategies in this book you're setting yourself up for disappointment.

Here are a few things you shouldn't expect from fundraising from businesses.

- It won't replace individual gifts or grants as the biggest drivers of funds to your organization.
- It won't "save your nonprofit" if you are in dire financial straights.
- It won't last forever. The majority of your business partners will come and go based on marketing objectives, support (or lack of it) from senior management, or economic conditions. Expect your partnership to have a shelf life—and an expiration date.

Miracles do happen—like the two college students that worked with a t-shirt company after the Boston bombings and raised $1 million for the victims (see Chapter 32), but you shouldn't plan on one.

PUT YOUR BOXING GLOVES ON

Ten years ago I had to explain to businesses what fundraising for a cause was all about, how it worked, and how they would benefit. Today, businesses know all about working with causes. The bigger challenge for nonprofits is to convince a business to add you to the mix of nonprofits they support, or to switch their support to you.

Here's how to position your organization for success when you have competition.

Stress your local roots. The *2010 Cone Cause Evolution Study*, which you can download at Cone.com, reported that 91 percent of respondents think companies should support an issue in the communities where they do business. People love good causes all over the world, but home is where the heart is.

Show companies how your nonprofit is making a difference in the community where their employees work and where consumers are buying their products or services.

Be as transparent as possible. More than ever, donors want nonprofits to be as open as possible about how funds are spent and how much is supporting the mission. Local nonprofits have a great advantage on this front as donors can see firsthand where their money is going.

Instead of giving their money to nonprofits halfway across the country, or the world, show companies that they have a trusted partner right in their own backyard.

Give it all away. I have a saying, "Free is for me." Whether it's a nonprofit or a business, everyone loves free. Not charging a partner a fee, or not asking them to pick up the expenses of a fundraiser, gives you a competitive edge over other nonprofits that do. By *giving it all away*, you remove the number one reason why businesses say no. More importantly, your nonprofit gains a lot more than it loses.

Let's use the example of pinups (Chapter 15). Say that a grocery-store chain agrees to host a pinup fundraiser in 15 stores. Based on the customer traffic in these stores, you estimate you'll raise, on average, $500 per store, per week for four weeks. If you pay 10 cents for each pinup sold during that period, it will cost you $50 per store, per week to supply the pinups. Your total expense will be $3,000. But during that same period you'll raise $30,000.

Now, ask yourself, is it better to find a business that's willing to cover your expenses, or is it easier and better to give the pinups away and recruit a new partner that can easily raise five-figures?

You don't even have to be good at math to know the answer to this question!

Service, service, service. In addition to giving it all away, you should offer to do all the work, too. After money, businesses will worry that a fundraiser will require too much time and effort. Remove that as an obstacle by offering to do everything that isn't directly related to them raising money for your organization.

Again, let's use the example of pinups (Chapter 15). Your job is to design, print, and ship the pinups. You should also create an incentive program for employees and customers to boost your success. Of course, your business partner should be involved in finalizing the pinup design and approving employee incentives. But you—not they—are doing the work.

Your business partner has one job: to sell pinups at the register and raise money for your organization. *Give them the one job you can't do and is critical to the success of the fundraiser.*

Target businesses that already support charities. A friend of mine who used to sell advertising always told me that it was a hundred times easier to sell advertising to someone who was already buying it.

"The problem with new advertisers is that they've already made up their mind that they don't need advertising," he explained. "It's almost impossible to convince them otherwise."

The same may be true of businesses that have never supported a nonprofit. In this day and age when supporting a cause is the "must do" thing for businesses, those businesses that don't may think they can't or shouldn't. Convincing them otherwise may not be worth the effort.

The point is to go where you are loved, and a business that already supports a charity is more likely to fall in love with you than a business that has never supported one.

GET PROFESSIONAL HELP

It's not easy to find the right person to help you raise money from businesses. This is the case for a couple of reasons.

First, few people have experience with the strategies outlined in this book. Sure, people can learn on the job, but I'm amazed at the money that nonprofits will spend while they wait for results. They're reinventing the wheel, which is totally unnecessary.

Second, say that you do find someone with business-giving experience, which probably means they've worked for one of the larger nonprofits. Maybe they worked at Feeding America or Komen for the Cure or the American Cancer Society. These are big institutions with multimillion-dollar fundraising programs.

But here's the dirty secret: These people know little about how to start, grow, and market a business fundraising program for an organization that isn't a brand heavyweight.

These people are talented project managers, for sure, but their field is service, not sales. They're great when a company comes calling with their 5,000 store locations and seven-figure advertising budget. But they're not so good when it comes to starting a program and selling companies from a cold start.

I've talked to these shell-shocked people shortly after they've started with "Average Joe Nonprofit" and this is what they say.

"No one calls me back."

"My board isn't helpful."

"I have to do everything myself."

"No one knows who we are."

"All the companies I call are already working with a major charity."

"This is the hardest thing I've ever done in my life."

'You bet it's hard! That's why most nonprofits that are serious about raising money from businesses shouldn't start by hiring a full-time fundraiser. They should hire an agency or consultant instead. It will cost more money in the beginning, but you'll see better results and ultimately raise more money, which will offset the expense.

If you need some suggestions on agencies and consultants that might be a good fit for your organization, e-mail me at joe@selfishgiving.com.

I said in the preface that for me inspiration is everything. If I've done my job, this book has inspired you to roll up your sleeves and tackle fundraising with businesses.

Fortunately, I'm leaving you with more than a full head of steam. Thanks to my blog, Selfishgiving.com, the book hashtag #fwb40 and my Pinterest boards, you'll enjoy a steady stream of advice, examples, case studies and, yes, more inspiration to guide you.

This isn't the last chapter. It's only the end of the first chapter. For those of you who want to join me, we'll write the next chapters together.

About the Author

Joe Waters (from Boston, Massachusetts) has been working at the intersection of business, philanthropy and marketing for 20 years. He writes one of the web's leading fundraising blogs, Selfishgiving. com. He's the author of *Cause Marketing for Dummies*.

Index